فَيْضُ احَرَمِ فِي آدَابِ الْمُطَالَعَةِ

The Outpouring of the Sacred Precinct

A Manual on the Art of Reading

فَيْضُ الْحَرَمِ فِي آدَابِ الْمُطَالَعَةِ

The Outpouring of the Sacred Precinct

A Manual on the Art of Reading

Authored by

SHAYKH AḤMAD IBN LUṬFULLĀH

With Forewords by

DR. JONATHAN A. C. BROWN

DR. SHADEE ELMASRY

Translated by

MIKAEEL AHMED SMITH

Contents

THE OUTPOURING OF
THE SACRED PRECINCT
A MANUAL ON THE ART OF READING

Acknowledgements

Our beloved Prophet Muhammad ﷺ has conveyed to us a tradition that is based on thankfulness and appreciation. When questioned about his ﷺ reasons for standing in the middle of the night hour upon hour, the Prophet ﷺ replied:

"Shall I not be a grateful servant?"

I would like to take this opportunity to express my extreme gratitude to all those who have contributed to the translation of this text and helped facilitate what you hold before you. Firstly, I would like to thank my beloved friend, Rushain Abbasi, without whom I would have never stumbled upon the original manuscript.

Secondly, Dr. Edmund Tori, whose suggestions regarding productivity and efficiency made this work a reality during my many bouts with writer's block. I would also like to thank Dr. Tori's daughter, Aasiya Tori, who worked hour after hour putting together the initial draft. This work would not be here today were it not for my beloved brother and friend, Adil Sayyidi (Justin Cole), and his careful review and assistance with the text. I would like to thank my beloved wife who is a constant inspiration for me. Lastly, I would like to thank Muhammad Sattaur and Imam Ghazali Publishing for their support and assistance in bringing this work to fruition. All success is from Allah alone.

اقْرَأْ بِٱسْمِ رَبِّكَ ٱلَّذِى خَلَقَ ۞

Publisher's Message

THE PRECIOUS HERITAGE OF ISLAMIC KNOWLEDGE

In the year 96 AH, the Umayyad Caliph ʿUmar ibn ʿAbd al-ʿAzīz wrote to the scholars of Madinah with an urgent command: "Look for the knowledge of Hadith and write it down, for I fear that knowledge will vanish and the scholars will pass away." This moment marks a pivotal transformation in Islamic civilization, when the preservation of sacred knowledge moved from oral tradition to written word. The command was both practical and prophetic, recognising that each generation bears responsibility for transmitting the intellectual and spiritual heritage of Islam to those who follow.

The book you hold represents a remarkable link in this unbroken chain of knowledge transmission. Written in the sacred precinct of Makkah over three centuries ago, *Fayḍ al-Ḥaram* addresses a perennial challenge that faces every serious student of Islamic sciences: how does one truly read, understand, and retain sacred knowledge? The author's insights, penned while sitting before the Kaʿbah, speak across centuries to address our contemporary struggles with depth, attention, and authentic learning.

THE AUTHOR AND HIS HISTORICAL CONTEXT

Shaykh Aḥmad ibn Luṭfullāh lived during one of Islamic history's most fascinating periods, serving as Chief Astronomer to Sultan Mehmed IV, who ruled the Ottoman Empire from 1648 to 1687. This was an era when Istanbul stood as perhaps the world's greatest centre of learning, where scholars from across the Muslim world gathered to advance every field of knowledge from astronomy to jurisprudence. The Ottoman Empire during this period represented the height of Islamic institutional learning, with elaborate scholarly hierarchies, rigorous certification processes, and vast libraries that preserved centuries of Muslim intellectual achievement.

Sultan Mehmed IV's reign, though politically tumultuous, witnessed remarkable intellectual productivity. The sultan himself maintained close relationships with scholars, as evidenced by his appointment of Shaykh Aḥmad to the intimate position of *Muṣāḥib-i-Pādishāhī*, placing him within the ruler's innermost advisory circle. This proximity to power gave the author unique insights into how knowledge functions at the highest levels of civilisation, where learning serves not merely individual enrichment but the guidance of an entire empire.

The author's life journey from Salonika to Istanbul, then to Egypt in exile, and finally to residence in Makkah and Madinah, provided him with exposure to the full breadth of Islamic scholarly traditions. He studied under masters in the Mawlawiyyah tradition, engaged with Egyptian scholars, and ultimately chose to spend his final years in the holy cities, where he passed away in 1702 near the grave of our mother Khadījah ﷺ. This geographic and intellectual journey enriched his understanding of how knowledge is acquired, transmitted, and preserved across different Muslim contexts.

THE CIVILIZATIONAL MOMENT AND ITS RELEVANCE

The late seventeenth century, when Shaykh Aḥmad wrote this treatise, was a period of profound transformation in the Muslim world. Traditional methods of education were encountering new challenges: the proliferation of written texts was changing how students engaged with knowledge, the expansion of the Ottoman bureaucracy was creating new demands for standardised education, and scholars were increasingly concerned about maintaining depth and authenticity in an era of rapid change. The author's worry that students were becoming satisfied with superficial reading, losing the ability to extract deeper meanings from texts, resonates powerfully with our current moment.

Today, we face remarkably similar challenges amplified by digital acceleration. The abundance of information available at our fingertips has paradoxically made deep understanding more elusive. Students can access thousands of classical texts online yet struggle to properly comprehend even one. The traditional teacher-student relationship that once guaranteed proper understanding has been disrupted, leaving many seekers to navigate complex scholarly works alone. This context makes Shaykh Aḥmad's systematic approach to self-study not merely relevant but essential for contemporary students.

THE UNIQUE VALUE OF THIS WORK

What distinguishes *Fayḍ al-Ḥaram* from other works on seeking knowledge is its technical precision. While numerous classical texts address the spiritual and ethical dimensions of learning, few systematically analyse the cognitive processes involved in deep reading. The author breaks down the act of studying into its constituent elements: understanding individual words, grasping grammatical structures, recognising rhetorical devices, identifying logical arguments, and synthesising complex meanings into coherent understanding. He addresses practical questions rarely discussed in classical literature: How does one know if they have truly understood a text? What are the signs of superficial versus deep comprehension? How can a student without access to teachers verify their understanding?

The work is particularly valuable for intermediate students who have moved beyond basic literacy but have not yet achieved scholarly mastery. The author explicitly states his audience: those who are "gradually proceeding through the stages of perfection by increasing day by day, little by little." This precise targeting makes the book immediately practical for serious students who find themselves between elementary instruction and advanced scholarship.

THIS SECOND EDITION: OUR RENEWED COMMITMENT

When we first published *Fayḍ al-Ḥaram* in 2017, Imam Ghazali Publishing was primarily focused on teaching rather than full-time publishing. The translation, while sincere, was undertaken without the resources and expertise that such a significant text deserved. As we have grown into a dedicated publishing house, we recognised our responsibility to revisit this important work and give it the careful attention it merits.

This second edition represents a complete reimagining of the text. Every sentence has been rebuilt from the ground up, with the English reviewed for accuracy and clarity. We returned to the Arabic manuscript, catching errors and ambiguities missed in the first edition. The transliteration system has been standardised with full diacritics according to our style guide, ensuring consistency and scholarly precision. Chapter headings have been clarified to better guide readers through the author's systematic approach, and we have added contextual notes about the Ottoman period to help readers understand the civilisational moment of the text's composition.

The new edition benefited from extensive testing with teachers and students in traditional learning environments. Their feedback helped identify passages needing clarification and concepts requiring additional context for contemporary readers. This collaborative approach ensures the book serves its intended purpose as a practical guide for serious students. Our evolution as publishers has taught us that presenting classical texts requires not just translation but careful adaptation that maintains authenticity while ensuring accessibility.

The need for this book has only intensified since our first edition. The COVID-19 pandemic forced a global experiment in remote learning, revealing both the possibilities and pitfalls of education without direct teacher supervision. Many Muslims discovered during this period their hunger for serious engagement with classical texts, yet also their lack of preparation for independent study. Social media has created new venues for Islamic learning but also new confusions, as students struggle to distinguish between scholarly depth and superficial popularisation.

The author's warnings about the dangers of hasty reading and intellectual superficiality speak directly to our moment. His observation that students often move "from one idea to the next, even with only the smallest amount of association between the two ideas" perfectly describes the hyperlinked, attention-fractured nature of contemporary digital reading. His insistence that true understanding requires sustained focus, systematic progression, and patient repetition offers a methodology for reclaiming depth in an age of distraction.

Furthermore, the democratisation of access to Islamic texts through digital libraries and online repositories makes the book's guidance crucial. When anyone can download the entirety of *Ṣaḥīḥ al-Bukhārī* or *Iḥyāʾ ʿUlūm al-Dīn*, the question becomes not access but approach. How does one read these monuments of Islamic scholarship without a teacher's guidance? How can students avoid the misunderstandings that arise from encountering complex texts without proper preparation? These questions make *Fayḍ al-Ḥaram* indispensable for contemporary seekers.

This book invites readers into a tradition that views reading not as passive consumption but as active transformation. The Islamic concept of *muṭālaʿah* that the author expounds encompasses more than moving one's eyes across a page. It involves engaging all one's faculties, from grammatical analysis to logical evaluation, from rhetorical appreciation to spiritual reception. The goal is not merely to acquire information but to be transformed by knowledge, to move from understanding to realisation, from learning to becoming.

We publish this second edition with the prayer that it will serve a new generation of students who hunger for authentic engagement with their intellectual heritage. The author's systematic approach offers a middle path between the impossibility of traditional apprenticeship for many contemporary students and the dangers of unguided self-study. His methods, tested across centuries, provide practical tools for those who seek to drink deeply from the wellsprings of Islamic knowledge.

As publishers, we see our role as facilitators in this sacred process of knowledge transmission. By presenting this text with the care and precision it deserves, we hope to honour both the author's legacy and our readers' sincere pursuit of learning. May this book serve as a bridge connecting contemporary seekers to the vast ocean of Islamic scholarship, providing not just information but transformation, not just understanding but realisation.

The journey of knowledge that began with the divine command *"Iqra'"* continues in every generation through those who take seriously their role as inheritors of prophetic wisdom. This book stands as testimony that the methodologies for pursuing sacred knowledge remain as relevant today as they were when the author sat in contemplation before the House of Allah, pouring his insights onto paper for the benefit of students he would never meet but whose struggles he intimately understood.

MUHAMMAD SATTAUR
Imam Ghazali Publishing

Foreword

FIRST FOREWORD, BY DR. JONATHAN A. C. BROWN

For those who spend significant parts of their professional or personal lives engaged with the Islamic intellectual tradition, with hours passed scanning page after page or pondering one page in depth, there are questions that not only go unanswered but oddly most often go unasked. For me, the most pressing is how the scholars who produced the voluminous works of Hadith, *tafsīr, fiqh*, language and history could possibly have taken in, digested and reproduced such vast quantities of information. Even in the modern day, with the aid of computers, databases and the internet, just trying to keep up with their work can occupy a scholarly career. How did those hundreds and hundreds of Muslim scholars who produced just the largest books in Islamic civilisation go about studying, memorising, looking up and referencing the ocean of details that they so skilfully sailed with such seeming ease? Every once in a while there are tantalising hints: children in West Africa writing and rewriting the words of the Qur'an and, later, beginning books of law in charcoal on planks of wood; al-Ḥāfiẓ Ibn Ḥajar mentioning how he wrote the *Fatḥ al-Bārī* by gathering a team of senior students, assigning each certain subjects to research and then meeting regularly with them to bring their contributions together. I wish I knew more about how these scholars undertook those feats of the mind and memory that daunt me daily in my own research.

Shaykh Aḥmad ibn Luṭfullāh's *Fayḍ al-Ḥaram*, translated here, provides a glimpse into how pre-modern Muslim scholars conceptualised the process of reading, understanding, retaining and employing knowledge. In that sense it is a valuable historical artefact for those interested in Islamic intellectual history. It offers a relatively rare reflection, considered self-criticism, and proposed solution to what the author felt were challenges facing students in his milieu. But the work is also useful across the many centuries that separate us from its author. It gives valuable lessons on how we think about reading, critically examining and classifying information. May God grant benefit to its author, translator and to us all through it.

Foreword

SECOND FOREWORD, BY DR. SHADEE ELMASRY

This text offers guidance for a situation in which many students of knowledge find themselves today. Namely, reading works in the *sharīʿah* sciences without access to teachers. This book is for the intermediate student who has grasped certain *uṣūlī* and logical concepts that help in understanding the degrees of certainty on which evidences and proofs are built. In the shaykh's words: "that student who is gradually proceeding through the stages of perfection by increasing in his studies day by day, little by little. This is what is intended by the term, 'intermediate student', or 'one who is between the beginner and the expert.'" In terms of genre, this book should be read after *Treatise for the Seeker of Knowledge* by Imam al-Muḥāsibī, which covers the *adab* and manners of one who is about to begin his journey in *ṭalab al-ʿilm* (seeking knowledge).

The Arabic of this text was not easy. I would rate it as difficult, even more so in manuscript form, and because of that, students of knowledge should be very grateful that Shaykh Mikaeel Smith has been able to deftly translate it and present it in accessible English. This effort is also a testament to Shaykh Mikaeel's scholarship and grasp of the language.

I would like to highlight three simple, yet critical points that the author ﷺ brings up. In this sense, my contribution to this publication serves as a type of summary of the benefits of this work. The three points are:

1. Why the study of *dīn* requires more caution than any other discipline.
2. The danger of self-study.
3. The guidelines for self-study.

The reader must know that the author, Shaykh Aḥmad ibn Luṭfullāh, an Ottoman scholar who took residence in Makkah, has brought up many more useful and interesting analyses such as: the essential elements of thought and thinking, the causes of stupidity, the tension between memorising and thinking, the dangers of boredom and when one should stop reading, and the need for tranquillity for the mind to function sharply.

WHY THE STUDY OF THE DĪN REQUIRES CAUTION

Disciplines are treated with as much caution as the missteps therein are dangerous. Misquoting a poet has very little "real" consequences. Writing a bad novel has no negative impact on anyone except the author and the status of his income. As such, the field of literature is wide open for whomever attempts to access it; it has no certification board. Now consider bridge-building, flying planes or surgery, and the matter is completely different. There is no room for incompetent people to slip through the cracks of those fields and endanger people's lives. The dīn is one thousand times more critical than these disciplines. What people believe about the universe provides the foundations for a society's approach to all other fields, sciences, laws, customs and cultures. In addition to these worldly realities, errors in theology, as Imam al-Shāfiʿī noted, can initiate a series of events that ends with Hell-Fire, eternal or otherwise.

Consider the case of Barsīṣā the monk as an example. He made the fatal error of imagining that spiritual inspirations (ilhām) were superior to revealed textual knowledge. Shayṭān then wielded this against him, making him fall into the deadly trap of arrogance over the ʿulamāʾ, which led to distance from them, which in turn cut him off from knowledge. In time, Barsīṣā found himself entangled in an affair with a woman that resulted in pregnancy. Fearing the loss of his reputation as a saintly worshipper, he killed the woman. Fearing to be caught as a murderer, he obeyed Shayṭān, who appeared to him with a deal: "bow down to me and I will extricate you from this impending scandal." At the end of a prolonged drama, the one-time saintly devotee to God ended his life having submitted to Iblīs. But the beginning of the drama was one simple error in knowledge, namely failing to recognise that textual knowledge takes precedence over spiritual inspiration without invalidating the latter as a source of clarification for the former. The slander of the ʿulamāʾ collectively is in fact a slander of the religion itself and cuts one off from the greatest sabab (material cause) of salvation: sacred knowledge.

Barsīṣāʾs case may sound extreme, but that is only due to the extremes of saintliness, adultery, murder and the manifestation of Shayṭān. In essence, the idea of going astray into kufr is not uncommon at all. Consider how many thousands (if not millions) of believers were lost due to a similar error, namely that of Mirza Ghulam, a man whose beginning was in the circles of knowledge and whose end was in the claim to prophecy. He attracted a large following of believers and took them from claim to claim until he and they ended up in disbelief. Worse, they coalesced into a formal community which resulted in their offspring also living and dying in the same kufr. How many lineages of īmān were cut off by one man's delusions? Every renegade and heretical sect began with one man who may have simply suffered one misstep in theology. This is why the field of sacred knowledge is so sensitive and must be treated with the utmost care and caution.

Today, we find ourselves in a moment filled with critical thinkers, authors, speakers and activists that can amplify their voices and spread their ideas, while not necessarily appreciating the sanctity and sensitivity of theology and the grave consequences of errors therein. Well-intentioned influencers may end up spreading misguidance without even realising it.

Allah tells us, "Shall I not tell you about the worst failures in their deeds? Those whose efforts were in misguidance, thinking they were doing good" (18:103-4). Worse, the mere idea of a dichotomy of guidance vs misguidance is often mocked. As a result, we find ourselves in the "Wild Wild West" of Islamic thought, where no identifiable majority, university or canon can be found to offer any measure of stability. This is all the more reason for us to emphasise knowledge and, equally important, the process of its acquisition.

THE DANGER OF READING BY ONESELF

As a general rule, reading the technical sciences of *sharīʿah* without an experienced person to explain it is extremely dangerous for a number of reasons, logical and spiritual. Firstly, imagining that one has understood a text does not necessarily mean that they have in fact understood it as the author intended. In reading *Ṣaḥīḥ Muslim* with my teacher, we would come upon many Hadiths that were widely circulated and known. Further, we would spend much time reading the various chains and narrations of those Hadiths. I shared an idea with the shaykh: why don't I read the chapter myself at home, then simply put a mark next to the Hadiths that I didn't understand. The shaykh replied, "I'm not worried about what you don't understand; I'm worried about what you think you understand." We continued to go over every expression and meaning, and it was an exercise in respect for the text which was a symbol of the tradition as a whole.

The number of errors that a person can make reading on their own is unfathomable. To give an example, as soon as you buy a book, you are essentially vouching for the veracity of the publisher without even realising it. One is engaged in an act of *taqlīd*, blindly believing that the publisher was honest and accurate in their transmission. Publishing houses of Islamic texts should be treated with the same critical eye as transmitters of Hadith. If the book is a translation, then it is double the effect, since translation itself is a form of interpretation, which is essentially scholarship. And so, before you have even opened the book, you have placed your religion in the hands of people you have no information about, without even knowing it. This is why one's initial knowledge acquisition must be through living human beings whom the family or community have assessed and vouched for.

The second harm has to do with cutting off from the *jamā'ah*. Let us suppose, hypothetically, that an advanced student could read without misunderstanding. He or she knows the technical terms, studied logic and *uṣūl* and benefits perfectly from their books. They would still be deficient from another angle, namely that of the added benefits of the traditional person-to-person method of studying: the idea of *ṣuḥbah*. Self-study, even if extremely successful, can have the negative side-effect of cutting one off from the *jamā'ah*. Why go to a class when I can read it myself in a shorter time from the comfort of my own home? Keeping the company of scholars is not solely about ensuring the accuracy of our understanding. It is also about maintaining pious company, which offers spiritual re-invigoration, moral reminders, exhortations and *naṣā'iḥ*, and a strengthening of one's defences against Shayṭān, who finds it easy to pick off the lone sheep but immensely difficult to attack a *jamā'ah*. A scholar alone may understand without error, but is nonetheless a fallible human being susceptible to the whisperings of Shayṭān, who will work on his morals and behaviour tirelessly until he slackens in observance. Good company protects from this.

The third type of harm is of a spiritual nature. The idea of seeking teachers and consulting one's peers has a spiritual effect, namely eradicating *kibr*. It has been said that no one becomes a scholar until they have studied with their elders, their peers and those younger than them. When they do this, they have proven their respect for the discipline over their love for their ego and its being superior to those of his generation, for the ego has no problem honouring the achievements of deceased scholars but has great reservation in respecting its peers. Asking others is a humbling experience, in which one is essentially admitting ignorance on a matter. The refusal to corroborate one's understanding with a peer or someone younger can only be based in arrogance and *kibr*.

THE GUIDELINES FOR READING BY ONESELF

At what point can a student begin reading technical works independently? The author spends most of the book addressing this question. The summary answer revolves around the student's grasp over the following:

1. The different sources of knowledge.
2. The different types of evidences (speculative vs absolute, general vs specific, etc.).
3. The structure of a sound argument (firmly establishing sound premises that lead to a conclusion).

Knowledge is derived from four sources: revelation, transmission, reason and observation (revelation in fact is a branch of transmission). If a student is firm in their epistemology, they will avoid many pitfalls, the worst of which is *kufr* and the least of which is the wastage of time. Oftentimes, I come upon questioners whose *īmān* has been shaken by the latest scientific theory. In such cases, I never discuss the theory. Rather, I begin explaining epistemology and the difference between direct observations and the theories that explain those observations. Scientific theories are never true or false. Rather, they are merely valid so long as they do not contradict any other evidences. But for believers, we also require the theory not to contradict revelation. No matter how impressive a theory is, be it scientific, historical, economic, or otherwise, if it contradicts unequivocal revelation (i.e. a verse or verified Hadiths whose meanings cannot be differed upon), then the learned believer rejects them on epistemic grounds. We must say: the Qur'an is right and the theory will eventually be disproven by evidence that has yet to be discovered. (Avid supporters of a theory are also resting on faith, namely the belief that contradictory evidence will not be discovered). As soon as a piece of information reaches the student of knowledge, he or she places it in one of the above categories: is it revelation? Is it a historical transmission? Human reason? Observation?

Within revelation, not all of its texts are equal. Among the verses are, as Allah says, "cornerstones of the Book, while others are ambiguous (mutashābihāt)." Ibn ʿAbbās classifies verses into: "those which have only one meaning, and those that have multiple meanings." The second source, the Sunnah, itself contains various types. Between the mutawātir Hadith, the ṣaḥīḥ and ḥasan Hadiths, the ʿamal of Madinah, the fatāwā of the Companions, and the action of the Companions, there is much discussion and debate among the mujtahid imams. Many fail to recognise that the ṣaḥīḥ Hadith has limits in the Ḥanafī madhhab (it cannot offer an exception to the Qur'an), while it is superseded by the ʿamal of Madinah in the Mālikī madhhab. After the Sunnah comes qiyās (analogy), ijmaʿ (consensus) and numerous other tools and the vast discussions that surround them. A strong basis in uṣul is a requirement in avoiding confusion.

After understanding the types of evidences and the system of deriving rulings, there is the structure of the argument itself. This is a sub-branch of manṭiq (logic). The biggest error in this regard is the conflation between "evidence" and "proof". Every text available is a piece of evidence, but that evidence must be built into a solid proof. It is much like a crime scene, in which the police gather the evidences, while the prosecutor weaves the evidences into a case. A sound argument posits two or more absolutes that necessitate a conclusion.

In addition to these fundamentals of *fiqh*, essential for self-study, Shaykh Aḥmad also gives practical advice. Among them is his warning that "digressing from one thing to the next is harmful because the one who does so becomes accustomed to a lack of attention." When a student chooses a book to read, after consulting with their teachers and peers about it, they should focus on it and should not be diverted. Every time the thought comes to divert, he should ask, "what was my original intention?" If your initial decision turned out to be wrong, then how do you know that this decision is not also wrong? In this case, the person needs to go deeper and reassess their decision-making process. A teacher of mine once said, "The best book you read is the one you finish." Wandering from book to book, reading half a chapter here and half a chapter there is acceptable for leisurely or secondary knowledge, but not for the essential sciences of their chosen discipline, such as *fiqh*. For such works, the student is best off labouring through one book, not grazing through many. "The primary cause for students not reaching perfection is hastiness and impatience... The primary cause of this is one's desire to raise their status in the sight of people and to gain acceptance from them." We also know that Shayṭān himself will introduce the seeker to something good only to divert him from the good that he is already upon, so that he never completes anything. We ask Allah *ʿāfi-yah* and *salāmah* from this.

CONCLUSION

Sacred knowledge is a delicate enterprise; the stakes are very high. In addition to caution in how we study, there must also be caution in how knowledge affects us, i.e. vigilance when it comes to arrogance, *kibr* and relying on our own abilities.

As the intention of this foreword has been to summarise the shaykh's arguments and extract its benefits, I close by sharing some of his counsels:

"The student should travel from one continent to the next, seeking out teachers and scholars and not become impressed with himself or herself and their own ability. One should never desist from seeking more knowledge through taking it from the mouths of perfected teachers... going directly to them and seeking the benefit that is gained by sitting with perfected scholars, meeting them, and keeping their company. That benefit is one which can never be obtained by mere study.

In regard to others, the student should have high opinions, both of those preceding the student, and those that live in the same time, seeing in them perfection and superiority, never looking down upon anyone because of their speech or apparent understanding.

One should instead hold a sceptical opinion of one's self. One must be very careful to not become deluded by their own understanding and mental acumen. This will lead to him or her refraining from seeking out knowledge and participating in gatherings of knowledge. He or she will thus rely solely on their own ability to study.

Lastly, one must be completely and absolutely careful to avoid bad manners in regard to one's pious predecessors because this is a major cause of one being deprived of reaching perfection.

We ask Allah for noble enablement and for good manners with our pious predecessors and our peers at all times."

Āmīn.

Translator's Preface

All praise belongs to Allah, the Lord of the worlds. May peace and blessings be upon our master Muhammad ﷺ, his family, and his companions all together. About ten years ago while rummaging through my mother's library, I came across an old book with an eye-catching title. Underestimating my mother's taste in literature, I had no idea that I was holding an original copy of one of the most widely-read books on education, *How to Read a Book by Mortimer Adler*.

At that time, I was studying in a traditional Islamic seminary and immediately recognised the value of this book. As I read through it, I fell in love with how the author taught the art of reading. Reading is an art, a skill, and most certainly a science. I grabbed the book and informed my mother I needed to borrow it and take it to the *madrasah*. "Boy, you better bring back my book!" she exclaimed as I stuffed it into my bag. Book lovers know the struggle is real when it comes to lending books.

After reading the book cover to cover multiple times, I knew that the book was a literary masterpiece. However, I wondered if Islamic scholarship outlined and codified the science of reading prior to this. My question was answered two years ago while I was researching Islamic pedagogical thought. I happened to come across an original Arabic manuscript from the twelfth century *hijrī* written by the Chief Astronomer of Sultan Mehmet IV, titled *Fayḍ al-Ḥaram fī Ādāb al-Muṭālaʿah* or in English, "Enlightenment from the Sacred Precinct: A Manual on the Art of Reading". To my surprise, the work had never been translated into any other language, nor had it been published in Arabic. *Fayḍ al-Ḥaram* stands in history as a unique gem that, until now, remained a lost treasure of intellectual thought in Islamic pedagogy.

Since the dawn of revelation upon the blessed Prophet Muhammad ﷺ, generations of Muslims have held learning and education to be a noble act of worship. Prophetic traditions enumerating the status of scholars are countless and well-known to all Muslims. The final message to mankind revealed upon Prophet Muhammad ﷺ simply began, "read!", and the command has echoed in the ears of countless students and teachers, inspiring an Islamic pedagogical system that emphasises the culturing of man through education and learning. Islamic pedagogy strives for ethical and academic excellence, and this work is a small example of Islamic pedagogical thought and its detail.

Shaykh Aḥmad ibn Luṭfullāh penned this book towards the end of his life. Sitting in front of the Kaʿbah, he wrote the text with the intention that it may serve as a source of revival of the deep analytical Islamic tradition in matters of education. Shaykh Aḥmad was a polymath, having mastered multiple sciences where he was considered an official authority. He is known to have authored books in history, maths, and astronomy.

He states in the beginning of this great work that his main motivating reason for writing the text was the lack of attention given to the proper manner of perusing books, or *muṭālaʿah*. His primary goal here is to teach and preserve the concept of "deep reading". It is my belief that deep reading of the classical religious texts has not only wavered but, in essence, died in many of today's schools. It could indeed be argued that studies are dedicated to a ceremonial teaching of books. *Fayḍ al-Ḥaram* is a fresh reminder about the classical scholarly approach to learning.

Until now, students of Islamic seminaries who searched for texts devoted to a correct method of knowledge acquisition would encounter books that focused heavily on the *adab*, or manners and etiquettes, of acquisition. This includes how one should walk, eat, and stack books in proper order. While we hold these principles in the highest regard, a student in today's context is heavily in need of a manual for the actual methods of reading and knowledge acquisition. In my understanding, the author's fear of a paradigm shift of the Islamic educational system away from critical analysis to a mere reading of the text has been realised. We have lost contact with the actual objectives of the trivium, and important sciences like logic are merely glossed at, at best. The author views the method of knowledge acquisition equally important as the content itself. The Islamic scholastic tradition is from one perspective anti-autodidact, giving extreme importance to formal education under a qualified scholar. The pedagogical methods that were spoken about by the Shaykh ultimately strive to create within a student a sort of readiness, or *istiʿdād*, for independent acquisition of any science.

MIKAEEL AHMED SMITH
Maryland, USA
November 10, 2016

Author's Biography

All praise belongs to Allah, the Lord of the worlds. May peace and blessings be upon our master Muhammad ﷺ, his family, and his companions all together. *Fayḍ al-Ḥaram* was written in the later years of Shaykh Aḥmad ibn Luṭfullāh's life, in the year of 1691 CE, after he had been removed from his position as Chief Astronomer and exiled to Egypt. Shaykh Aḥmad ibn Luṭfullāh was born in Salonika, Greece. His father, Luṭfullāh, left his small Turkish town of Ereğli to begin a new life in Greece. Within a few years, Luṭfullāh would be blessed with a baby boy whom he named Aḥmad, born in the year 1631. From an early age, Shaykh Aḥmad was attached to the circles of knowledge. Sitting with the likes of Shaykh ʿAbdullāh, the grand *muftī* of Salonika, he excelled in Arabic, Islamic law, Prophetic traditions, and Qurʾanic exegesis.

By the year 1654, he was ready to further his education. He travelled to Istanbul, where he studied under multiple teachers in various fields. He studied philosophy, metaphysics, and logic under Shaykh Ṣāʾib Effendi. He also studied under the leading astronomer of Istanbul, Muḥammad Effendi. He spent the majority of his time studying and learning under the supervision of a spiritual guide, Shaykh Khalīl Dede, in the Mawlawiyyah *zāwiyah*. It is here that the reality of Islamic scholarship was realised for Shaykh Aḥmad, for he began to understand a well-known tradition that, "the scholars are the inheritors of the Prophets". The spiritual reality of knowledge should be transferred into the heart of its possessor during the stages of knowledge acquisition. This is the ultimate objective of studying.

اقْرَأْ بِاسْمِ رَبِّكَ الَّذِي خَلَقَ

"Read! In the name of your Lord."

His intellectual strength and spiritual depth caught the eye of many in Istanbul. Upon the death of Chief Astronomer Muḥammad Shalabī in 1667, Shaykh Aḥmad was assigned to take up his post by Sultan Mehmed IV. It is clear that Sultan Mehmed IV held the Shaykh in high regard, eventually honouring him with the position of *Muṣāḥib-i-Pādishāhī* and thus entering him into the innermost circle of the Sultan. When Sultan Mehmed IV was removed from his post in November 1687, Shaykh Aḥmad ibn Luṭfullāh was forced into exile in Egypt, where his adopted son Morālī Ḥasan Pasha served as governor.

After some time, Shaykh Aḥmad moved to Makkah, where he became the spiritual leader of the local Mawlawiyyah *zāwiyah*. He moved to Madinah between 1693 and 1694 where he stayed for seven years. In 1700, he was recalled to Istanbul to resume work as the Chief Astronomer, however declined the position due to concerns regarding his age. He returned to Makkah for a final time, where he passed away on 27 February 1702 CE (30 Ramadan 1113 AH). His tomb is located near the grave of our mother Khadījah ﷺ.

فَيْضُ الْحَرَمِ فِي آدَابِ الْمُطَالَعَةِ

The Outpouring of
the Sacred Precinct

A Manual on the Art of Reading

Authored by

SHAYKH AḤMAD IBN LUṬFULLĀH

With Forewords by

DR. JONATHAN BROWN

DR. SHADEE ELMASRY

Translated by

MIKAEEL AHMED SMITH

Author's Preface

All praise is due to Allah ﷻ who created man with the ability to study all the apparent aspects of existence and enabled him to contemplate His manifest signs. Thereafter, praise is due to Allah ﷻ for blessing mankind with the jewel of intellect so that they may be guided by it. By this, mankind may attain that which is unknown by means of the known. Peace and blessings be upon the most complete of those who studied, the most observant, our master Muhammad ﷺ, the seal of the Prophets and Messengers. Peace and blessings be upon his family and his companions, who shined due to observing his splendour and due to being guided by his perfection ﷺ. May prayers be upon him constantly, and upon his companions and family.

Thereafter, this servant, seeking the bounty of his mighty Lord ﷻ, Aḥmad ibn Luṭfullāh al-Mawlawī, may Allah ﷻ forgive and manifest kindness on him and his parents, begins with the following:

My heart was troubled for some time. My mind continued to think of how previous scholars, may Allah ﷻ grant them coolness in their graves, had such an abundance of love and mercy for seekers of sacred knowledge. They did not neglect any beneficial advice that would facilitate for them the means and methods of knowledge acquisition. They expounded in great detail upon all things that guide a student to his or her goal, whilst providing scrupulous details of the ultimate reality. From this effort they codified the rules of debate and discussion, allowing both topics to develop into independent sciences. Additionally, they authored many works in the sciences of debate and discussion and expounded on existing texts with their commentaries and marginal notes. However, we find that scholars have yet to write exclusively on the manners and etiquettes of knowledge acquisition. Furthermore, the methods and levels of knowledge acquisition have never been

بِسْمِ اللَّهِ الرَّحْمَنِ الرَّحِيمِ

صَلَّى اللهُ عَلَى مُحَمَّدٍ وَآلِهِ وَصَحْبِهِ وَسَلَّمَ

الْحَمْدُ للهِ الَّذِي جَعَلَ الْإِنْسَانَ مُسْتَعِدًّا لِمُطَالَعَةِ الْكَائِنَاتِ مَعَ مَا فِيهَا مِنَ النُّقُوشِ الظَّاهِرَةِ، وَلِمُلَاحَظَةِ الْمَصْنُوعَاتِ وَمَا فِيهَا مِنَ الْآيَاتِ الْبَاهِرَةِ، وَشَرَّفَهُ بِجَوْهَرِ الْعَقْلِ لِيَسْتَدِلَّ بِهِ مِنَ الْعَرَضِ الْمَحْسُوسِ عَلَى الْجَوْهَرِ الْمَعْقُولِ، وَيَتَّصِلَ بِإِعْدَادِهِ مِنَ الْمَعْلُومِ إِلَى الْمَجْهُولِ، وَالصَّلَاةُ وَالسَّلَامُ عَلَى أَكْمَلِ الْمُطَالِعِينَ وَأَفْضَلِ الْمُلَاحِظِينَ سَيِّدِنَا مُحَمَّدٍ خَاتَمِ الْأَنْبِيَاءِ وَالْمُرْسَلِينَ وَآلِهِ وَصَحْبِهِ الْمُتَشَرِّفِينَ بِمُطَالَعَةِ جَمَالِهِ، الْمُتَأَدِّبِينَ بِآدَابِ كَمَالِهِ، دَامَتِ الصَّلَاةُ عَلَيْهِ وَعَلَى صَحْبِهِ وَآلِهِ.

أَمَّا بَعْدُ: فَيَقُولُ الْعَبْدُ الْوَاثِقُ بِفَضْلِ رَبِّهِ الْقَوِيِّ أَحْمَدُ بْنُ لُطْفِ اللهِ الْمَوْلَوِيُّ، غَفَرَ اللهُ لَهُ وَلِوَالِدَيْهِ وَأَحْسَنَ إِلَيْهِمَا وَإِلَيْهِ: قَدْ كَانَ يَخْتَلِجُ فِي صَدْرِي، وَيَتَرَدَّدُ فِي خَلَدِي أَنَّ الْعُلَمَاءَ السَّالِفِينَ بَرَّدَ اللهُ مَضْجَعَهُمْ مَعَ كَثْرَةِ شَفَقَتِهِمْ وَسَعَةِ مَرْحَمَتِهِمْ فِي حَقِّ الطَّالِبِينَ حَيْثُ لَمْ يُهْمِلُوا شَيْئًا مِمَّا يُسَهِّلُ طُرُقَ التَّحْصِيلِ عَلَيْهِمْ إِلَّا بَيَّنُوهُ بِدَقَائِقِهِ وَلَمْ يَتْرُكُوا أَمْرًا مِمَّا يُعِينُهُمْ فِي الْوُصُولِ إِلَى الْكَمَالِ إِلَّا ذَكَرُوهُ بِحَقَائِقِهِ حَتَّى دَوَّنُوا آدَابَ الْمُنَاظَرَةِ وَالْمُبَاحَثَةِ وَجَعَلُوهَا عِلْمًا بِرَأْسِهِ وَأَلَّفُوا فِيهِ كُتُبًا كَثِيرَةً مِنَ الْمُتُونِ وَالشُّرُوحِ وَالْحَوَاشِي. فَمَا مَنَعَهُمْ مِنْ ذِكْرِ آدَابِ الْمُطَالَعَةِ وَتَدْوِينِهَا عِلْمًا كَآدَابِ الْمُنَاظَرَةِ مَعَ كَوْنِ الْأُولَى أَهَمَّ مِنَ الثَّانِيَةِ فِي حَقِّ الطَّالِبِينَ؛ لِأَنَّ الْمُنَاظَرَةَ مُتَوَقِّفَةٌ عَلَى الْمُطَالَعَةِ؛ إِذْ كُلُّ مُنَاظَرَةٍ لَمْ تَسْبِقْهَا مُطَالَعَةٌ لَا تُنْتِجُ سِوَى الْمُجَادَلَةِ وَالْمُخَاصَمَةِ، فَلَا تُثِيرُ غَيْرَ الْخَجَالَةِ وَالنَّدَامَةِ.

codified. For the student of knowledge, knowing the art of acquisition and identifying its levels are more important than knowing the science of debate; debate is dependent upon one's ability to study. Every debate not preceded by proper study and research is merely argument and disputation, resulting only in embarrassment and prolonged regret.

One may suggest that the early scholars left this area to the understanding of the student, and trusted that one would learn the proper methods of acquiring knowledge from the actions and examples of those who came before them. Had this been true, it would have been more suitable for the early scholars to avoid mentioning the methodology of debate. Not only is it less important than the methodology of study and research, but it is also easier to learn and master. Their love and regard for students of sacred knowledge was far too great for them to merely leave this important art for the student to learn on their own. In the end, everything is left to Allah ﷻ and He alone controls the time in which all should happen.

While I was in this state of indecisiveness, I came across a passage where one of the early scholars mentioned some aspects of the methods of study, with the majority of the stated principles being taken from the methodology of debate. However, it was not sufficient to cure the one in need, nor to quench the thirst of the thirsty. Thus, I annotated the work with some of what I had learnt from my own teachers and scholars. It then occurred to me that I should put together a short treatise which discussed the methodology of study and the acquisition of knowledge along with its conditions in a way that would assist the student in their journey and aid the seeker in their research.

However, a few things prevented me from pursuing this. Firstly, my nights were disrupted by much preoccupation due to changing circumstances in my life. Secondly, I noticed a lack of zeal in today's students of knowledge and a restriction of

فَإِنْ قِيلَ: تَرَكُوهَا إِحَالَةً عَلَى فَهْمِ الطَّالِبِ وَاعْتِمَادًا عَلَى أَخْذِهِ تِلْكَ الْآدَابَ - أَعْنِي آدَابَ الْمُطَالَعَةِ - مِنْ صَنِيعِ السَّلَفِ فِي آثَارِهِمْ مِنَ الشُّرُوحِ وَالْحَوَاشِي؛ إِذِ الْمُطَالَعَةُ إِمَّا فِي الْمَتْنِ أَوْ فِي الشُّرُوحِ وَالْحَوَاشِي.

قُلْتُ: لَوْ كَانَتْ تَرْكُهُمْ لِمَا قِيلَ لَكَانَتْ آدَابُ الْمُنَاظَرَةِ بِالتَّرْكِ أَوْلَى وَأَنْسَبَ مِنْ آدَابِ الْمُطَالَعَةِ؛ لِأَنَّهَا مَعَ كَوْنِهَا أَحَطَّ رُتْبَةً فِي اللُّزُومِ مِنْ آدَابِ الْمُطَالَعَةِ أَظْهَرُ مِنْهَا وَأَسْهَلُ أَخْذًا مِنْ صَنِيعِ الشُّرَّاحِ وَأَصْحَابِ الْحَوَاشِي؛ مَعَ أَنَّ كَثْرَةَ الشَّفَقَةِ تُنَافِي الْإِحَالَةَ وَتَأْبَى عَنِ الْحَوَالَةِ.

وَالْجَوَابُ الشَّافِي: أَنَّ الْأُمُورَ كُلَّهَا بِيَدِ اللهِ وَهِيَ مَرْهُونَةٌ بِأَوْقَاتِهَا.

وَبَيْنَمَا أَنَا فِي هَذَا التَّرَدُّدِ إِذْ صَادَفْتُ طُرْفَةً قَدْ جَمَعَ فِي مِقْدَارِ صَحِيفَةٍ ضَمَّنَهَا أَحَدٌ مِنَ الْعُلَمَاءِ الْمُتَأَخِّرِينَ عِدَّةَ كَلِمَاتٍ مُتَعَلِّقَةٍ بِآدَابِ الْمُطَالَعَةِ وَكَانَ أَكْثَرُهَا مَأْخُوذًا مِنْ آدَابِ الْمُنَاظَرَةِ لَكِنَّهُ مِنْ قَبِيلِ مَا لَا يَشْفِي الْعَلِيلَ وَلَا يَرْوِي الْغَلِيلَ فَكَتَبْتُ عَلَيْهِ شَيْئًا مِمَّا اسْتَفَدْتُهُ مِنْ آثَارِ الْعُلَمَاءِ وَأَخَذْتُهُ مِنْ أَفْوَاهِ الْفُضَلَاءِ. وَخَطَرَ بِبَالِي أَنْ أَجْمَعَ مُخْتَصَرًا يَحْتَوِي عَلَى آدَابِ الْمُطَالَعَةِ وَشَرَائِطِهَا عَلَى وَجْهٍ يُفِيدُ الطَّالِبِينَ تَرَقِّيًا فِي مُطَالَعَاتِهِمْ، وَيُعْطِي الْمُحَصِّلِينَ كَمَالًا فِي مُلَاحَظَاتِهِمْ، ثُمَّ مَنَعَنِي مِنْ هَذِهِ الْخَاطِرَةِ عِدَّةُ أُمُورٍ:

مِنْهَا: تَشَتُّتُ الْبَالِ لِكَثْرَةِ الِاشْتِغَالِ وَانْقِلَابِ الْأَحْوَالِ.

وَمِنْهَا: مُلَاحَظَةُ قُصُورِ الْهِمَمِ فِي الطَّالِبِينَ، وَمُشَاهَدَةُ مَا هُمْ عَلَيْهِ مِنْ قَصْدِ الطَّلَبِ عَلَى مَا يَرْغَبُ فِيهِ عَوَامُّ النَّاسِ مِنَ الْحَشْوِيَّاتِ وَالدَّنْدَنِيَّاتِ.

their focus to that which is lowly. Thirdly, and perhaps the most hindering of all, was that I noticed my own limitations. I said to myself:

> "Oh you poor and incapable man! Have you attained the level of writing and authoring? There is indeed an added challenge to writing in a genre where no one has preceded you with anything of benefit. Nor does there exist any written work to aid you in that which is difficult or that which is hidden from you."

Much time passed in this state. I would begin at one point and then become overwhelmed by the task at hand. This condition continued until Allah ﷻ rectified my state by blessing me with closeness to the sacred precinct. Additionally, I was requested by some of the people of wisdom and nobility to embark on this endeavour. Due to the blessing of being in proximity to the sacred precinct and the truthfulness of the request, I overcame my hesitation and, relying on Allah's ﷻ help, the King, the All-Knowing, I began to compile a short treatise regarding the methodology of study.

This treatise contains a preface, five sections, and a conclusion. While writing, I continually begged Allah ﷻ to bring it to a good end. I named it *Fayḍ al-Ḥaram* so that it may be known that the production of this book was not by any ability of my own, but only by the benevolence of Allah ﷻ and His gift. We ask by His inclusive grace and magnificent generosity that we make it for His noble sake, and that He make it beneficial for seekers of knowledge. We further ask that this will be a provision for us on the Day of Resurrection, by the sanctity of all the Prophets and Messengers, may the peace of Allah ﷻ be upon them all.

وَمِنْهَا: مَا هُوَ أَمْنَعُ الْمَوَانِعِ أَنِّي لَاحَظْتُ قِلَّةَ بِضَاعَتِي وَعَدَمَ اسْتِطَاعَتِي فَقُلْتُ لِنَفْسِي: أَيُّهَا الْعَاجِزُ الْمِسْكِينُ أَيْنَ أَنْتَ وَأَيْنَ رُتْبَةُ التَّأْلِيفِ وَالتَّصْنِيفِ؟ سِيَّمَا تَقُولُ التَّأْلِيفُ فِيهِ قَرِيبًا مِنَ الْإِبْدَاعِ وَالِاخْتِرَاعِ؛ حَيْثُ مَا سَبَقَكَ أَحَدٌ فِيهِ بِتَأْلِيفٍ مُفِيدٍ وَلَا بِتَصْنِيفٍ مَنِيعٍ حَتَّى تَسْتَعِينَ بِهِ فِيمَا صَعُبَ عَلَيْكَ وَتَسْتَكْشِفَ عَنْهُ فِيمَا خَفِيَ لَدَيْكَ.

وَمَضَى عَلَيَّ زَمَانٌ وَأَنَا فِي هَذَا التَّرَدُّدِ أُقَدِّمُ تَارَةً وَأُحْجِمُ أُخْرَى حَتَّى جَمَعَ اللهُ شَمْلِي بِأَنْ شَرَّفَنِي بِجِوَارِ بَيْتِهِ الْحَرَامِ، وَضَمَّ إِلَى الدَّاعِيَةِ الْمَذْكُورَةِ طَلَبَ بَعْضِ الْأَذْكِيَاءِ الْكِرَامِ؛ فَبِبَرَكَةِ الْجِوَارِ وَصِدْقِ الطَّلَبِ تَرَجَّحَ الْإِقْدَامُ عَلَى الْإِحْجَامِ، وَشَرَعْتُ فِي جَمْعِ الْمُخْتَصَرِ الْمَذْكُورِ مُسْتَعِينًا بِاللهِ الْمَلِكِ الْعَلَّامِ، وَرَتَّبْتُهُ عَلَى مُقَدِّمَةٍ، وَخَمْسَةِ مَقَاصِدَ، وَخَاتِمَةٍ، وَذَيْلٍ؛ سَائِلًا مِنَ اللهِ حُسْنَ الْخِتَامِ. وَسَمَّيْتُهُ فَيْضَ الْحَرَمِ لِيَشْعُرَ بِأَنَّ ظُهُورَهُ لَيْسَ بِالِاسْتِعْدَادِ؛ بَلْ بِمُجَرَّدِ الْفَيْضِ وَالْإِنْعَامِ. وَالْمَسْؤُولُ مِنْ فَضْلِهِ الْعَمِيمِ وَكَرَمِهِ الْعَظِيمِ أَنْ يَجْعَلَهُ خَالِصًا لِرِضَائِهِ الْكَرِيمِ، وَأَنْ يَجْعَلَهُ نَفْعًا لِلطَّالِبِينَ وَذُخْرًا لَنَا فِي يَوْمِ الدِّينِ بِحُرْمَةِ سَيِّدِ الْأَنْبِيَاءِ وَالْمُرْسَلِينَ وَصَلَوَاتُ اللهِ عَلَيْهِ وَعَلَيْهِمْ أَجْمَعِينَ.

Author's Introduction

To begin, one must know the actual meaning of *muṭālaʿah*, or studying, which includes both the lexical and terminological meaning. The lexical meaning of the word *muṭālaʿah* is to look at something. Generally, it is commonly used by the scholars to mean looking over or reviewing a written work, seeking to gain a deeper understanding of it or of something dependent on it. Furthermore, it means to look over written words whose meanings are known, seeking to reach that which was intended explicitly by the author, or that which is plausible. Studying is a science. It addresses the etiquettes of research and investigation along with the conditions of both. Its subject matter is the terminological meaning of *muṭālaʿah*.

Ultimately, the benefit is to protect the mind of the student from limiting themselves to the outward meanings of written works, and to prevent one from being deprived of the true realities and intricacies of a written work. The benefit of this knowledge is to use these etiquettes to increase one's ability to derive meanings from something. As for the objectives of knowledge acquisition, they are four. They vary according to the level of the student:

The student at the beginner's stage has a good introductory knowledge of that which they intend on studying but does not have practically applicable knowledge of it. For such a student, the objective is that they gain this practical knowledge.

The student at the next level has practical knowledge in relation to that which they are studying, although this knowledge is one of imitation. He or she has not learnt from the perspective of proofs. Their objective while studying is that they should solidify that knowledge by understanding it through proofs.

الْمُقَدِّمَةُ

فِي أُمُورٍ تُعِينُ مَعْرِفَتُهَا فِي مَعْرِفَةِ الْمَقْصُودِ

[تَعْرِيفُ الْمُطَالَعَةِ وَمَبَادِئُهَا]

مِنْهَا، مَعْرِفَةُ الْمُطَالَعَةِ لُغَةً وَاصْطِلَاحًا: اعْلَمْ أَنَّ الْمُطَالَعَةَ فِي اللُّغَةِ بِمَعْنَى الِاطِّلَاعِ، يُقَالُ: طَالَعْتُهُ طِلَاعًا وَمُطَالَعَةً أَيِ اطَّلَعْتُ عَلَيْهِ. وَأَمَّا فِي الِاصْطِلَاحِ أَعْنِي فِي عُرْفِ عَامَّةِ الْعُلَمَاءِ عَلَى مَا يُفْهَمُ مِنْ مَوَارِدِ اسْتِعْمَالِهِمْ إِيَّاهَا فَبِالْإِجْمَالِ: «مُلَاحَظَةُ الْمَرْسُومِ لِتَحْصِيلِ الْمَفْهُومِ» وَبِالتَّفْصِيلِ: «مُلَاحَظَةُ الْأَلْفَاظِ الْمَرْسُومَةِ، الْمَعْلُومَةِ الْوَضْعِ لِمَعَانِيهَا؛ لِلتَّوَصُّلِ بِهَا إِلَى مَا قُصِدَ بِإِيرَادِهَا مِنْ بَيَانِ حَقِيقَةٍ أَوْ إِثْبَاتِ مَطْلَبٍ، عَلَى وَجْهٍ مُعْتَبَرٍ عِنْدَ أَصْحَابِ التَّحْقِيقِ». فَهُوَ عِلْمٌ يُبْحَثُ فِيهِ عَنْ آدَابِ الْمُطَالَعَةِ وَشَرَائِطِهَا. وَمَوْضُوعُهُ: الْمُطَالَعَةُ الِاصْطِلَاحِيَّةُ. وَغَايَتُهُ: صَوْتُ الذِّهْنِ عَنِ الِاقْتِصَارِ عَلَى الظَّوَاهِرِ، وَالْحِرْمَانُ مِنَ الْحَقَائِقِ وَالدَّقَائِقِ.

وَالْفَائِدَةُ مِنْهُ: هِيَ التَّرَقِّي فِي اسْتِخْرَاجِ الْمَعَانِي مِنَ الْعِبَارَاتِ بِمُرَاعَاةِ تِلْكَ الْآدَابِ. وَأَمَّا الْغَرَضُ مِنْ نَفْسِ الْمُطَالَعَةِ فَمُنْحَصِرٌ فِي أَرْبَعَةٍ بِاعْتِبَارِ مَرَاتِبِ الْمُطَالِعِينَ؛ لِأَنَّ الْمُطَالِعَ أَيِ الَّذِي لَهُ حَظٌّ وَنَصِيبٌ مِنِ اسْتِخْرَاجِ الْمَعَانِي مِنَ الْعِبَارَاتِ بِمُجَرَّدِ مُلَاحَظَتِهِ وَنَظَرِهِ فِيهَا لَا يَخْلُو:

[١] إِمَّا أَنْ يَكُونَ مِمَّنْ لَهُ اسْتِعْدَادٌ قَرِيبٌ بِالنِّسْبَةِ إِلَى الْمَحَلِّ الَّذِي يُطَالِعُ فِيهِ وَلَيْسَ لَهُ بِهِ عِلْمٌ بِالْفِعْلِ، فَغَرَضُهُ مِنَ الْمُطَالَعَةِ أَنْ يُحَصِّلَ ذَلِكَ الْعِلْمَ أَيِ الْعِلْمَ بِالْفِعْلِ.

[٢] وَإِمَّا أَنْ يَكُونَ لَهُ عِلْمٌ بِالْفِعْلِ بِالنِّسْبَةِ إِلَى الْمَحَلِّ الْمُطَالَعِ فِيهِ؛ لَكِنْ

The student at the next level has solidified knowledge in relation to what they are studying. However, they are deficient in knowledge retention. Their objective while studying is that they reach a higher level by repeating that which they have received.

The student at the final level has acquired, verified, and retained knowledge through studying, but such knowledge can be increased. Their objective in studying is that they increase their ability and let it grow by taking it from many places to strengthen their practical ability.

From this, we see there are four objectives of studying: to acquire, to verify, to retain, and to increase and strengthen one's knowledge. For each one of these objectives of study there are special etiquettes, just as there are general etiquettes of studying which will strengthen and help each of the categories. Accordingly, I have made the chapters of this work corresponding to these five categories. As for the benefit of this knowledge, there is something for every person who finds themselves on the path of study; however, the majority of benefit will be for the common seeker of knowledge.

A student seeking perfection in knowledge will be one of three levels: the beginner, the intermediate, and the expert learner. A seeker is in the beginning stages of knowledge when they are unaware of the methodology of studying and the methodology of deriving meanings from written works. The student at this level of learning should primarily take what they are seeking from the mouths of teachers because they are merely a beginner. As far as the one who has reached the later stages of studying, they have obtained and perfected the ability to easily derive the deeper meanings of things presented to them without much mental exertion. This is the level of the expert seeker of knowledge. As for the intermediate student, he or she has gained the ability to derive meanings, however, this ability is neither completed nor perfected.

تَقْلِيدِيٌّ لَيْسَ بِمَأْخُوذٍ مِنَ الدَّلِيلِ، فَغَرَضُهُ مِنَ الْمُطَالَعَةِ أَنْ يُحَقِّقَ ذَلِكَ الْعِلْمَ بِأَخْذِهِ مِنَ الدَّلِيلِ.

[٣] فَإِمَّا أَنْ يَكُونَ لَهُ عِلْمٌ تَحْقِيقِيٌّ بِالنِّسْبَةِ إِلَيْهِ؛ لَكِنَّهُ لَيْسَ فِي مَرْتَبَةِ مَلَكَةِ الِاسْتِحْضَارِ، فَغَرَضُهُ مِنَ الْمُطَالَعَةِ أَنْ تُوَصِّلَهُ إِلَى تِلْكَ الْمَرْتَبَةِ بِتَكْرَارِ أَخْذِهِ مِنَ الْمَآخِذِ.

[٤] وَإِمَّا أَنْ يَكُونَ لَهُ عِلْمٌ تَحْقِيقِيٌّ؛ لَكِنَّهُ مِمَّا يَقْبَلُ الزِّيَادَةَ وَالْقُوَّةَ، فَغَرَضُهُ مِنَ الْمُطَالَعَةِ أَنْ يَزِيدَ عَلَيْهِ فَيُنَمِّيَهُ أَوْ يَأْخُذَهُ مِنْ مَآخِذَ كَثِيرَةٍ فَيُقَوِّيهِ.

فَعَلَى هَذَا تَكُونُ الْأَغْرَاضُ مِنْ نَفْسِ الْمُطَالَعَةِ أَرْبَعَةَ أَقْسَامٍ: إِمَّا التَّحْصِيلُ أَوِ التَّحْقِيقُ أَوِ الِاسْتِحْضَارُ أَوِ التَّنْمِيَةُ وَالتَّقْوِيَةُ. وَلِكُلِّ نَوْعٍ مِنْ هَذِهِ الْأَنْوَاعِ الْأَرْبَعَةِ مِنَ الْمُطَالَعَةِ آدَابٌ خَاصَّةٌ بِهِ كَمَا أَنَّ لِمُطْلَقِ الْمُطَالَعَةِ آدَابًا عَامَّةً تَعُمُّ جَمِيعَ الْأَنْوَاعِ؛ وَلِهَذَا جُعِلَتْ مَقَاصِدُ هَذَا الْمُخْتَصَرِ مَبْنِيَّةً فِي خَمْسَةٍ.

وَأَمَّا نَفْعُ هَذَا الْفَنِّ فَيَعُمُّ جَمِيعَ مَنْ لَهُ حَظٌّ مِنَ الْمُطَالَعَةِ، إِلَّا أَنَّ نَفْعَهُ لِلْمُتَوَسِّطِ مِنَ الطَّلَابِ أَكْثَرُ. فَإِنَّ طَالِبَ الْكَمَالِ الْعِلْمِيِّ عَلَى ثَلَاثِ مَرَاتِبَ: مُبْتَدِئٌ وَمُنْتَهٍ وَمُتَوَسِّطٌ؛ لِأَنَّ الطَّالِبَ إِمَّا فِي أَوَائِلِ الطَّلَبِ لَيْسَ لَهُ نَصِيبٌ مِنَ الْمُطَالَعَةِ وَاسْتِخْرَاجِ الْمَعَانِي مِنَ الْعِبَارَاتِ بِمُلَاحَظَتِهِ؛ بَلْ هَمُّهُ أَنْ يَأْخُذَ مَطْلُوبَهُ مِنْ أَفْوَاهِ الرِّجَالِ، فَهُوَ «الْمُبْتَدِئُ». وَإِمَّا فِي آخِرِ الطَّلَبِ فَقَدْ حَصَلَتْ لَهُ مَلَكَةٌ تَامَّةٌ عَامَّةٌ يَسْتَخْرِجُ بِهَا الْمَعَانِيَ مِنَ الْعِبَارَاتِ الْوَارِدَةِ عَلَيْهِ بِسُهُولَةٍ مِنْ غَيْرِ تَكَلُّفِ رَوِيَّةٍ جَدِيدَةٍ، فَهُوَ «الْمُنْتَهِي». وَإِمَّا فِي أَوَاسِطِ الطَّلَبِ قَدْ حَصَلَتْ لَهُ مَلَكَةُ الِاسْتِخْرَاجِ؛ لَكِنَّهَا غَيْرُ كَامِلَةٍ يُرِيدُ تَكْمِيلَهَا بِالتَّتْمِيمِ وَالتَّعْمِيمِ فَهُوَ «الْمُتَوَسِّطُ».

Moving forward, know that the term "ability" is used to describe a deeply-rooted quality within a person. It is used to describe a type of conscientious effect that occurs with ease and without any deliberation. However, this is before the effect becomes a natural disposition; it is merely a temporal state which happens abundantly.

There are three levels that are sought after for the one seeking to perfect their knowledge. Each of these levels represents a stage in the acquisition of knowledge. The first stage is that of acquisition. This stage prepares a student for the next level: extrapolating meanings, which is the ability to deduce meaning. By means of the first stage, one can progress to the next: the deduction of knowledge. This capacity is obtained by learning the preliminary and introductory sciences of any field, and this is attained only through direct tutelage from a teacher. The goal and final objective of this capacity is to reach the next level, which is the capacity for the extrapolation of meanings. The first stage is the most general of all of the three abilities needed by a student.

The second stage is the ability to extract meanings; it is an ability by which an individual can derive meanings from anything they encounter. One should be able to do this with ease and without any deliberation or force. This stage is attained by the perfection of basic instrumental knowledge and by recalling the important topics discussed therein. The ability to extract meaning is completed and perfected when a student has gained, not only a mastery in the extrapolation of meaning, but an absolute certainty that what is obtained coincides with the real intent of the author.

This condition should be in regard to all or at least the majority of fields and sciences. The perfection of this condition will be obtained when two qualities are found in relation to the science: mastery, and confidence. This will be obtained by persistence and continuous study, taking into consideration

[الْمَلَكَةُ وَأَقْسَامُهَا]

اعْلَمْ أَنَّ الْمَلَكَةَ مُطْلَقًا عِبَارَةٌ عَنْ: كَيْفِيَّةٍ رَاسِخَةٍ فِي النَّفْسِ يَصْدُرُ بِهَا عَنِ النَّفْسِ نَوْعٌ مِنَ الْآثَارِ الِاخْتِيَارِيَّةِ بِسُهُولَةٍ مِنْ غَيْرِ رَوِيَّةٍ. وَيُقَالُ لَهَا قَبْلَ الرُّسُوخِ: «حَالٌ». وَهِيَ كَثِيرَةٌ؛ لَكِنَّ الْمَطْلُوبَ لِلْكَمَالِ الْعِلْمِيِّ ثَلَاثُ مَلَكَاتٍ مُرَتَّبَةٍ فِي الْحُصُولِ.

أُولَاهَا: «مَلَكَةُ الِاسْتِحْصَالِ»: وَهِيَ كَيْفِيَّةٌ رَاسِخَةٌ فِي النَّفْسِ تَسْتَعِدُّ بِهَا اسْتِعْدَادًا قَرِيبًا لِقَبُولِ الِاسْتِخْرَاجِ وَتَصْدُرُ بِهَا آثَارٌ مُلَائِمَةٌ لِمَرْتَبَةِ اسْتِعْدَادِ الِاسْتِخْرَاجِ. وَتَحْصُلُ هَذِهِ الْمَلَكَةُ بِأَخْذِ أَوَائِلِ الْعُلُومِ وَمَبَادِئِهَا الْأَوَّلِيَّةِ مِنْ أَفْوَاهِ الرِّجَالِ. وَغَايَتُهَا: حُصُولُ مَلَكَةِ الِاسْتِخْرَاجِ وَهِيَ أَعَمُّ الْمَلَكَاتِ الثَّلَاثِ.

وَثَانِيهَا: «مَلَكَةُ الِاسْتِخْرَاجِ»: وَهِيَ مَلَكَةٌ بِهَا تَسْتَخْرِجُ النَّفْسُ الْمَعَانِيَ مِنَ الْعِبَارَاتِ الْوَارِدَةِ عَلَيْهَا بِسُهُولَةٍ مِنْ غَيْرِ تَجَشُّمِ رَوِيَّةٍ. وَإِنَّمَا تَحْصُلُ هَذِهِ الْمَلَكَةُ بِإِتْقَانِ الْأُصُولِ مِنَ الْعُلُومِ الْآلِيَّةِ وَبِاسْتِحْضَارِ الْمُهِمَّاتِ مِنْهَا.

وَتُكْمَلُ بِأَمْرَيْنِ: أَحَدُهُمَا: أَنْ تَكُونَ النَّفْسُ فِي اسْتِخْرَاجِهَا بِهَا مُتَمَكِّنَةً مُطْمَئِنَّةً غَيْرَ مُتَرَدِّدَةٍ مُضْطَرِبَةٍ فِيهِ وَفِي مُطَابَقَتِهِ لِلْوَاقِعِ. وَثَانِيهِمَا: أَنْ تَكُونَ هَذِهِ الْحَالَةُ أَيِ التَّمَكُّنُ وَالِاطْمِئْنَانُ لِلنَّفْسِ عَامَّةً فِي جَمِيعِ الْعُلُومِ الْمُتَدَاوَلَةِ أَوْ فِي أَكْثَرِهَا. وَكَمَالُ هَذِهِ الْمَلَكَةِ بِهَذَيْنِ الْأَمْرَيْنِ أَيْ بِالتَّتْمِيمِ وَالتَّعْمِيمِ إِنَّمَا يَتَحَصَّلُ وَيَتَيَسَّرُ بِالْمُوَاظَبَةِ عَلَى الْمُطَالَعَةِ بِمُرَاعَاةِ آدَابِهَا وَشَرَائِطِهَا وَتَطْبِيقِ الْمُسْتَخْرَجِ بِهَا عَلَى مُسْتَخْرَجَاتِ الْكَامِلِينَ؛ إِمَّا بِمُشَافَهَتِهِمْ إِنْ وَجَدَهُمْ فِي عَصْرِهِ وَبَلَدِهِ، وَإِنْ لَمْ يَجِدْهُمْ فِي بَلَدِهِ يَخْتَارُ الرِّحْلَةَ إِلَيْهِمْ عَلَى سُنَنِ السَّلَفِ، وَإِنْ لَمْ يَجِدْهُمْ أَصْلًا لَا فِي بَلَدِهِ وَلَا فِي

all of the proper etiquettes and conditions of study. Thereafter, one should compare that which one has derived to the extrapolations of other people who have mastered this level of study, meeting them directly if they are accessible. Otherwise, they should travel to them, as this is the way of our pious predecessors. If you do not find such people in your town or elsewhere (as is the case in our time today), one should say to oneself, "verily we are from Allah ﷻ, and to Allah ﷻ do we return". Thereafter, one should study and follow their footsteps and correctly follow what they have written, and contemplate their actions as well as their methodologies of extrapolation. Similarly, one should focus on their method of distinguishing between one thing and another; how they entered into and concluded discussions, how they accepted and rejected certain matters, how they digressed during discussion in a way that did not deviate from the primary intent, and all of the other ways in which they conducted their investigation. From this method, one should gradually advance from a science to the one above it after he or she has perfected their ability to extract and deduce meanings with mastery and proficiency.

Due to the fact that the time it takes for one to perfect and master this capacity varies according to the acumen of the individual, scholars decided to set the time it would take for an intermediate student to read, under a master teacher, a certain set of books from various fields as a benchmark for obtaining and perfecting this quality.

Thereafter, scholars separated these sciences into introductory sciences and core subjects, naming the one who completed the core subjects *Mukammil al-Mawādd*, or "The Completer of Core Subjects". He or she is the one who has perfected and obtained the capacity to extrapolate meanings from those specific sciences completely. After reaching this stage, the student is no longer in need of a teacher. They should busy themselves

غَيْرِهِ كَمَا فِي عَصْرِنَا هَذَا كَذَلِكَ ـ إِنَّا لِلَّهِ وَإِنَّا إِلَيْهِ رَاجِعُونَ ـ فَبِمُتَابَعَةِ آثَارِهِمْ وَتَتَبُّعِ مُؤَلَّفَاتِهِمْ حَقَّ التَّتَبُّعِ وَبِالتَّأَمُّلِ فِي صَنِيعِهِمْ وَفِي كَيْفِيَّةِ اسْتِخْرَاجِهِمُ الْمَعَانِي مِنَ الْعِبَارَاتِ وَبَعْضِهَا مِنْ بَعْضٍ، وَفِي دُخُولِهِمْ فِي الْمَبَاحِثِ وَخُرُوجِهِمْ عَنْهَا، وَتَصَرُّفِهِمْ فِيهَا بِالرَّدِّ وَالْقَبُولِ، وَفِي تَشْعِيبِهِمُ الْكَلَامَ تَشْعِيبًا مَضْبُوطًا بِحَيْثُ لَا يَخْرُجُونَ بِهِ عَنِ الْمَقْصُودِ الْمَسُوقِ لَهُ الْكَلَامُ، وَغَيْرِ ذَلِكَ مِنْ آدَابِهِمْ فِي التَّخْرِيجِ. وَيَتَدَرَّجُ بِهَذَا الطَّرِيقِ مِنْ عِلْمٍ إِلَى آخَرَ فَوْقَهُ بَعْدَ أَنْ كَمُلَ اسْتِخْرَاجُهُ فِي الْأَوَّلِ بِالتَّمْكِينِ وَالتَّوْطِينِ.

وَلَمَّا رَأَى الْعُلَمَاءُ أَنَّ حُصُولَ هَذِهِ الْمَلَكَةِ وَكَمَالَهَا يَتَفَاوَتُ فِي الْأَزْمَانِ بِحَسَبِ تَفَاوُتِ الْأَذْهَانِ حَيْثُ تَحْصُلُ وَتُكْمُلُ لِلذَّكِيِّ فِي أَقْرَبِ الْأَزْمَانِ وَأَقْصَرِهَا وَلِلْبَلِيدِ فِي أَطْوَلِهَا وَأَبْعَدِهَا اعْتَبَرُوا زَمَانَ حُصُولِهَا وَكَمَالِهَا لِلْمُتَوَسِّطِينَ بَيْنَ الذَّكَاءِ وَالْغَبَاوَةِ، وَقَدَّرُوهُ بِزَمَانِ قِرَاءَةِ كُتُبٍ مِنْ عِدَّةِ عُلُومٍ مُتَدَاوَلَةٍ عَلَى أُسْتَاذٍ كَامِلٍ وَأَسَاتِذَ مَاهِرِينَ، وَقَسَّمُوا تِلْكَ الْعُلُومَ إِلَى مَبَادٍ وَ مَوَادٍّ، وَسَمَّوُا الْمُنْتَهَى بِهَا «مُكَمِّلَ الْمَوَادِّ».

وَهُوَ الْكَامِلُ الَّذِي حَصَلَتْ لَهُ مَلَكَةُ الِاسْتِخْرَاجِ مِنْ تِلْكَ الْعُلُومِ تَامَّةً عَامَّةً، وَكَمُلَتْ مِنَ الْجِهَتَيْنِ وَهُوَ لَا يَحْتَاجُ بَعْدَ ذَلِكَ إِلَى الْأُسْتَاذِ؛ بَلْ يَشْتَغِلُ بِتَنْمِيَةِ عِلْمِهِ وَتَقْوِيَتِهِ بِالْمُطَالَعَةِ وَالتَّكْرَارِ وَالْإِفَادَةِ.

with increasing their knowledge and strengthening it through study, repetition, and teaching.

The third ability to be sought after is the ability to recollect previously learnt knowledge easily; it is the ability by which one calls to recollection meanings and knowledge with ease, without any deliberation or force, and without the need to go back to the sources, be they books or individuals. This ability is mastered by repeatedly reviewing the respective sciences and their meanings until they are firmly and deeply established in one's mind to the fullest extent. This ability is completed when it is found regarding all sciences that are studied. However, it can also be held in regard to a certain specific science. This ability is the most rarified of all of the faculties, the highest of them in level, and the most difficult. When the term "expert" is used, it is referring to the one who has perfected this ability in all sciences, and in today's day and age, it is rarer than red sulphur. Similarly, when the term "master" is used in some sciences, it refers to the one who has the ability of recollection in that science, not the one who can extrapolate, nor the one who is at the stage of acquisition or obtaining knowledge. The usage of "master" for the one who can only extract meanings is figurative, in that the one who can extract meanings normally does so with the recollection of that knowledge. The seeker of knowledge should spend most effort in obtaining the ability to recollect their knowledge; they should not suffice with merely acquiring the ability to extrapolate meanings, even if this ability is perfected. This is because the master alone is the one who can recollect their knowledge.

There is no doubt that these three capabilities are sometimes in relation to just one question or topic. The first ability is that of acquisition. The second is the ability of extrapolation. The third is the ability of recollection and recall. As we have mentioned regarding the four levels of students, these three capabilities can be general or specific to one science. Here,

وَثَالِثَةُ الْمَلَكَاتِ الثَّلَاثِ الْمَطْلُوبَةِ «مَلَكَةُ الِاسْتِحْضَارِ»: وَهِيَ مَلَكَةٌ بِهَا تَسْتَحْضِرُ النَّفْسُ الْمَعَانِيَ وَالْعُلُومَ الْغَائِبَةَ عَنْهَا مَتَى شَاءَتْ بِسُهُولَةٍ مِنْ غَيْرِ تَكَلُّفِ رَوِيَّةٍ جَدِيدَةٍ وَلَا تَجَشُّمٍ مُرَاجَعَتِهَا إِلَى مَحَلِّهَا مِنَ الْكُتُبِ وَالرِّجَالِ. وَإِنَّمَا تَحْصُلُ هَذِهِ الْمَلَكَةُ بِتَكْرَارِ أَخْذِ الْمَعَانِي وَالْعُلُومِ مِنْ مَأْخَذِهَا حَتَّى تَتَمَكَّنَ وَتَتَقَرَّرَ فِي الذِّهْنِ تَمَكُّنًا بَالِغًا إِلَى الْغَايَةِ الْمَطْلُوبَةِ، وَتَكْمُلُ هَذِهِ الْمَلَكَةُ كَمَالًا حَقِيقِيًّا بِعُمُومِهَا فِي جَمِيعِ الْعُلُومِ الْمُتَدَاوَلَةِ، وَإِضَافِيًّا بِالنِّسْبَةِ إِلَى بَعْضِهَا. وَهَذِهِ الْمَلَكَةُ هِيَ أَخَصُّ الْمَلَكَاتِ وَأَعْلَاهَا رُتْبَةً وَأَعَزُّهَا وُجُودًا وَأَكْثَرُهَا رَغْبَةً فِيهَا. فَإِذَا أُطْلِقَ «الْكَامِلُ» صُرِفَ إِلَى صَاحِبِ هَذِهِ الْمَلَكَةِ فِي جَمِيعِ الْعُلُومِ، وَهُوَ فِي يَوْمِنَا هَذَا أَعَزُّ مِنَ الْكِبْرِيتِ الْأَحْمَرِ. وَكَذَا الْكَامِلُ بِالنِّسْبَةِ إِلَى بَعْضِ الْعُلُومِ كُلَّمَا ذُكِرَ يُرَادُ بِهِ الْمُسْتَحْضَرُ فِي ذَلِكَ الْعِلْمِ دُونَ الْمُسْتَخْرَجِ وَالْمُسْتَحْصِلِ. وَإِطْلَاقُ «الْكَامِلِ» عَلَى الْمُسْتَخْرِجِ التَّامِّ الْعَامِّ مَجَازٌ بِاعْتِبَارِ أَنَّ الِاسْتِخْرَاجَ التَّامَّ يُوجَدُ غَالِبًا مَعَ الِاسْتِحْضَارِ فِي أَكْثَرِ تِلْكَ الْعُلُومِ أَوْ مَعَ الِاسْتِعْدَادِ التَّامِّ لَهُ فِي جَمِيعِهَا.

فَيَنْبَغِي لِلطَّالِبِ أَنْ يَصْرِفَ هِمَّتَهُ فِي تَحْصِيلِ مَلَكَةِ الِاسْتِحْضَارِ فِي عُلُومِهِ وَلَا يَقْنَعُ عَلَى حُصُولِ مَلَكَةِ الِاسْتِخْرَاجِ وَلَوْ كَانَتْ تَامَّةً عَامَّةً؛ فَإِنَّ الْكَمَالَ هُوَ الِاسْتِحْضَارُ لَيْسَ غَيْرَ حَقِيقَةٍ، وَإِطْلَاقُ الْكَمَالِ عَلَى غَيْرِهِ مَجَازٌ بِاعْتِبَارِ كَوْنِهِ يَعْدِلُ الِاسْتِحْضَارَ.

وَلَا شَكَّ أَنَّ هَذِهِ الْمَلَكَاتِ الثَّلَاثَ قَدْ تَكُونُ بِالنِّسْبَةِ إِلَى مَسْأَلَةٍ وَاحِدَةٍ مَثَلًا تَحْصُلُ لِلشَّخْصِ بِالنِّسْبَةِ إِلَى مَسْأَلَةٍ وَاحِدَةٍ أَوَّلًا مَلَكَةُ الِاسْتِحْصَالِ ثُمَّ مَلَكَةُ الِاسْتِخْرَاجِ ثُمَّ مَلَكَةُ الِاسْتِحْضَارِ كَمَا قَالُوا بِمِثْلِ ذَلِكَ فِي الْمَرَاتِبِ الْأَرْبَعِ لِلْعَقْلِ: إِنَّهَا قَدْ تَكُونُ بِالنِّسْبَةِ إِلَى مُطْلَقِ الْعَقْلِ وَقَدْ تَكُونُ

what we refer to is its relationship to all sciences amongst the scholars. From this, it should become clear that the majority of benefit in this is for the student who is gradually proceeding through the stages of perfection by increasing in them day by day, little by little. This is what is intended by the term "intermediate student", or one who is between the beginner and the expert.

A student must also know the level of certainty and the speculative nature of the science they are studying. This facilitates successful attainment of their objective. Every student must have prior knowledge of the level of certainty and speculation that is possible for a particular science. This is so one does not seek out proofs for that which has no proofs, nor suffice with speculation in those areas where certainty is sought after.

The highest level of certainty lies in the science of engineering, because that which is produced from its premises is at the level of certainty and necessity. Thereafter are those knowledges which are gained by mathematical means, such as basic maths, surveying, algebra, balancing, astronomy, music, and others. The next level of certainty lies in the physical sciences and then the theological sciences. The physical sciences branch out to include medicine, astronomy and others, whereas the theological sciences, which are the highest form of speculative knowledge, branch out beyond theology and lay the foundations of jurisprudence.

After that, the sciences of grammar, etymology, and the derivation of words will be found. As for the science of language, there is a difference of opinion regarding it. Some claim that language is not a field of knowledge because it is merely a word for terminologies and definitions. I object to such a claim by stating that the science of language includes claims, therefore it is a knowledge. Some people refute my claim by stating that these claims are specific, whereas a knowledge must possess

بِالنِّسْبَةِ إِلَى بَعْضِ الْعُلُومِ؛ لَكِنَّ الْمُرَادَ مِنَ الْمَلَكَاتِ هُنَا هِيَ الَّتِي بِالنِّسْبَةِ إِلَى الْعُلُومِ الْمُدَوَّنَةِ الْمُتَدَاوَلَةِ بَيْنَ الْعُلَمَاءِ.

فَظَهَرَ مِنْ هَذَا التَّفْصِيلِ أَنَّ مُعْظَمَ الْمَنَافِعِ مِنْ هَذَا الْفَنِّ أَعْنِي مِنْ آدَابِ الْمُطَالَعَةِ إِنَّمَا هُوَ لِلطَّالِبِ الْمُتَدَرِّجِ فِي مَرَاتِبِ الْكَمَالِ بِاسْتِزَادَتِهِ يَوْمًا فَيَوْمًا شَيْئًا فَشَيْئًا. وَهَذَا الَّذِي يُعَبَّرُ عَنْهُ بِالتَّوَسُّطِ بَيْنَ الْمُبْتَدِي وَالْمُنْتَهِي؛ إِذِ الْمُرَادُ بِالْمُنْتَهِي هُنَا: مَنْ تَمَكَّنَ وَاسْتَقَرَّ فِي اسْتِخْرَاجِهِ فَيَكُونُ مُتَمَكِّنًا فِي آدَابِهِ الَّتِي اعْتَادَهَا فِي مُطَالَعَتِهِ وَمُلَاحَظَتِهِ فَيَكُونُ انْتِفَاعُهُ مِنْهَا قَلِيلًا.

[مَرَاتِبُ الْعُلُومِ]

وَمِمَّا يُعِينُ فِي الْمَقْصُودِ أَنْ يُعْرَفَ أَنَّ الْعُلُومَ مُتَفَاوِتَةٌ فِي مَرَاتِبِ الْيَقِينِ وَالظَّنِّ، فَيَجِبُ عَلَى كُلِّ طَالِبٍ أَنْ يَعْرِفَ مَرْتَبَةَ كُلِّ عِلْمٍ فِي الْيَقِينِ وَالظَّنِّ؛ لِئَلَّا يَطْلُبَ مِنْ أَدِلَّتِهِ مَا لَيْسَ فِي وُسْعِهَا أَوْ يَقْنَعَ بِالظَّنِّ فِي مَا يَجِبُ فِيهِ الْيَقِينُ.

فَفِي أَعْلَى مَرَاتِبِ الْيَقِينِ «عِلْمُ الْهَنْدَسَةِ»، فَإِنَّ الْمُسْتَفَادَ مِنْ بَرَاهِينِهَا يَقِينِيَّاتٌ فِي مَرْتَبَةِ الْأَوَّلِيَّاتِ وَالضَّرُورِيَّاتِ. ثُمَّ الْعُلُومُ الَّتِي يُسْتَدَلُّ فِيهَا بِأَدِلَّةٍ مُرَكَّبَةٍ مِنْ مُقَدِّمَاتٍ هَنْدَسِيَّةٍ مِثْلَ عِلْمِ الْحِسَابِ وَالْمِسَاحَةِ وَالْجَبْرِ وَالْمُقَابَلَةِ وَالْهَيْئَةِ الْمُسَطَّحَةِ الْمُبَرْهَنَةِ وَالْمُوسِيقِي الْمُسَمَّى بِعِلْمِ التَّأْلِيفِ وَغَيْرِهَا مِنْ فُرُوعِ الْهَنْدَسَةِ وَالْحِسَابِ.

ثُمَّ «الْحِكْمَةُ الطَّبِيعِيَّةُ»، ثُمَّ «الْإِلَهِيَّةُ»، وَمِنَ الْإِلَهِيَّةِ عِلْمُ الْكَلَامِ. ثُمَّ مَا يَتَفَرَّعُ عَلَى الطَّبِيعِيَّةِ مِثْلُ الطِّبِّ وَأَحْكَامِ النُّجُومِ وَغَيْرِهِمَا. ثُمَّ مَا يَتَفَرَّعُ عَلَى الْإِلَهِيَّةِ

general premises or claims. An answer to this counter-objection came to me, and perhaps it is not far from the truth: the science of language has in fact general claims, which are derived from examples, just like most of the Arabic sciences. This is supported by the fact that in every field of study from the aforementioned fields, there are general claims regarding language.

As far as lexicology is concerned, there is a difference of opinion regarding it as well. Some state that lexicology is not an independent science due to the fact that it consists of only terms and definitions. I respond to such a claim by saying that lexicology contains claims, and this shows that it is a type of knowledge. However, this claim of mine is refuted by some who say that these claims referred to in lexicology are specific premises, whereas knowledge is a term used for areas which have general premises. Consider this: every root word from the root words mentioned in the books of language is a general claim, and every possible derived word comes from these roots. The roots have set meanings that do not change. For example, *ḍaraba Zaydun*. Thereafter, those roots are used to derive other forms. For example, *ḍaraba, yaḍribu,* and *maḍrūb*. By this, we see that lexicology is a science that is speculative, and it is used to derive examples in etymology and areas other than that of the science of the Arabic language. We see that it is necessary for the student of knowledge to carefully consider seeking out that which is impossible, or sufficing with speculative knowledge where certainty can be achieved.

Among the sciences are also those in which no proof is sought at all. Rather, the utmost that is sought in them is the soundness of transmission, and they are accepted on the basis of good opinion, such as the science of history and literature. In these sciences, verification and scrutiny are possible through a method particular to them, which is learned by studying the books of literature and by repeatedly examining their poetry

وَهِيَ أَعْلَى مَرَاتِبِ الظَّنِّ عِلْمُ أُصُولِ الْفِقْهِ وَفُرُوعِهِ الْمُدَلَّلَةِ بِالْأُصُولِ ثُمَّ عِلْمُ النَّحْوِ ثُمَّ التَّصْرِيفِ وَالِاشْتِقَاقِ.

وَأَمَّا عِلْمُ اللُّغَةِ فَقَدِ اخْتُلِفَ فِيهِ، فَقَالَ بَعْضُهُمْ: إِنَّ اللُّغَةَ لَيْسَ بِعِلْمٍ؛ لِأَنَّهَا عِبَارَةٌ عَنِ التَّعْرِيفَاتِ اللَّفْظِيَّةِ. وَأُجِيبُ: بِأَنَّهَا تَتَضَمَّنُ دَعَاوَى، فَبِاعْتِبَارِهَا عِلْمٌ. وَرُدَّ: بِأَنَّ تِلْكَ الدَّعَاوَى قَضَايَا شَخْصِيَّةٌ، وَالْعِلْمُ عِبَارَةٌ عَنِ الْقَضَايَا الْكُلِّيَّةِ. فَخَطَرَ بِبَالِي جَوَابٌ لَعَلَّهُ غَيْرُ بَعِيدٍ وَهُوَ: أَنَّهَا دَعَاوَى كُلِّيَّةٌ مُسْتَدَلٌّ عَلَيْهَا بِالتَّمْثِيلِ كَمَا فِي أَكْثَرِ الْعُلُومِ الْعَرَبِيَّةِ. وَذَلِكَ أَنَّ فِي كُلِّ مَادَّةٍ مِنَ الْمَوَادِّ الْمَذْكُورَةِ فِي كُتُبِ اللُّغَةِ دَعْوَى كُلِّيَّةٌ، صُورَتُهَا: كُلُّ مَا يَتَرَكَّبُ مِنْ هَذِهِ الْمَادَّةِ الْمُرَتَّبَةِ مِثْلَ «ضَرَبَ زَيْدٌ» مَثَلًا فِي أَيِّ صُورَةٍ كَانَ، مَوْضُوعٌ بِمَعْنَى كَذَا مِثْلَ الْإِيجَاعِ وَالْإِيلَامِ. ثُمَّ يُسْتَدَلُّ عَلَيْهَا بِالْأَمْثِلَةِ الْجُزْئِيَّةِ الْوَارِدَةِ عَلَى صُوَرٍ شَتَّى مِثْلَ ضَرَبَ يَضْرِبُ وَمَضْرُوبٍ وَغَيْرِهَا، فَتَكُونُ دَعْوَى كُلِّيَّةٌ قَدِ اسْتُدِلَّ عَلَيْهَا بِجُزْئِيَّاتِهَا عَلَى طَرِيقِ التَّمْثِيلِ. وَعَلَى هَذَا يَكُونُ عِلْمُ اللُّغَةِ أَيْضًا مِنَ الْعُلُومِ الظَّنِّيَّةِ الْمُدَلَّلَةِ فِيهَا بِطَرِيقِ التَّمْثِيلِ، كَالتَّصْرِيفِ وَغَيْرِهِ مِنَ الْعُلُومِ الْعَرَبِيَّةِ.

فَيَجِبُ عَلَى الْمُطَالِعِ أَنْ يُرَاعِيَ مَرَاتِبَ الْعُلُومِ وَيُمَيِّزَ ظَنِّيَّهَا عَنْ قَطْعِيِّهَا حَتَّى لَا يُشْكِلَ الْأَمْرُ عَلَيْهِ إِمَّا بِطَلَبِ الْمُحَالِ أَوْ بِالْقَنَاعَةِ عَلَى الظَّنِّ فِيمَا يَجِبُ فِيهِ الْيَقِينُ.

وَمِنَ الْعُلُومِ أَيْضًا مَا لَا يُطْلَبُ فِيهِ الدَّلِيلُ أَصْلًا؛ بَلْ غَايَةُ مَا يُطْلَبُ فِيهِ صِحَّةُ النَّقْلِ، وَيُسَلَّمُ عَلَى سَبِيلِ حُسْنِ الظَّنِّ مِثْلُ عِلْمِ التَّارِيخِ وَالْمُحَاضَرَاتِ. وَفِيهِ يُمْكِنُ التَّحْقِيقُ وَالتَّدْقِيقُ بِجِهَةٍ مَخْصُوصَةٍ بِهِ تُسْتَعْلَمُ بِتَتَبُّعِ كُتُبِ الْأَدَبِ وَتَكْرَارِ النَّظَرِ فِي نَظْمِهِمْ وَنَثْرِهِمْ.

and prose. Among that which assists in achieving the objective is to know that every investigation has a beginning, a middle, and an end. Each of these has a necessary right that must be fulfilled.

As for the beginning: it is the claim or that which stands in its place. Its necessary right is that it be refined and clarified by specifying the intended meaning of every term and by specifying the position upon which the claim is built, so that mere verbal dispute does not occur.

As for the middle: it is the proof or that which stands in its place. This is the focal point of research and examination, and upon it revolves the question and answer. Its necessary right is that one contemplate its premises with due contemplation, and likewise its form and conditions as will be discussed, guarding against fallacy.

As for the end: it is the premise to which the discussion concludes and by which the intended compulsion and silencing of objection becomes manifest. Its necessary right is that its premise be self-evident, such as the impossibility of the conjunction of two contradictories or the negation of both together, the negation of a thing from itself, a thing preceding itself, contradiction of the assumption, the part being greater than the whole, circularity, infinite regress, and other such self-evident truths. Alternatively, the premise should be equivalent to self-evident truths by virtue of being accepted by the majority, such as the impermissibility of employing figurative speech without an indicator or recognised relation, or ellipsis before mention in both wording and rank, or other such accepted principles among the scholars of Arabic. The aforementioned right must be fulfilled, that the premise be self-evident or equivalent to it, so that the truth becomes manifest and the discussion concludes. We shall now proceed to the main objective and purpose, seeking assistance from Allah, the King, the All-Knowing.

وَمِمَّا يُعِينُ فِي الْمَقْصُودِ: أَنْ يُعْرَفَ أَنَّ لِكُلِّ مَبْحَثٍ مَبْدَأً وَوَسَطًا وَمَقْطَعًا. وَلِكُلِّ وَاحِدٍ مِنْهَا حَقٌّ لَازِمٌ يَجِبُ تَأْدِيَتُهُ. أَمَّا «الْمَبْدَأُ»: فَهُوَ الدَّعْوَى أَوْ مَا هُوَ بِمَنْزِلَتِهَا. وَحَقُّهُ اللَّازِمُ: أَنْ يُحَرَّرَ وَيُهَذَّبَ بِتَعْيِينِ الْمُرَادِ مِنْ كُلِّ لَفْظٍ وَبِتَعْيِينِ الْمَذْهَبِ الَّذِي يُبْنَى عَلَيْهِ الدَّعْوَى لِئَلَّا يَقَعَ النِّزَاعُ اللَّفْظِيُّ.

وَأَمَّا «الْوَسَطُ»: فَهُوَ الدَّلِيلُ أَوْ مَا هُوَ بِمَنْزِلَتِهِ. وَهُوَ مَحَطُّ رِحَالَةِ الْبَحْثِ وَالتَّفْتِيشِ، وَعَلَيْهِ يَدُورُ السُّؤَالُ وَالْجَوَابُ. وَحَقُّهُ اللَّازِمُ: أَنْ يُتَأَمَّلَ فِي مُقَدِّمَاتِهِ حَقَّ التَّأَمُّلِ، وَكَذَا فِي صُورَتِهِ وَشُرُوطِهِ كَمَا سَيَجِيءُ حَذِرًا عَنِ الْمُغَالَطَةِ.

وَأَمَّا «الْمَقْطَعُ»: فَالْمُقَدِّمَةُ الَّتِي يَنْتَهِي إِلَيْهَا الْكَلَامُ وَيَظْهَرُ بِهَا الْمُرَادُ مِنَ الْإِلْزَامِ وَالْإِفْحَامِ. وَحَقُّهُ اللَّازِمُ: أَنْ تَكُونَ مُقَدِّمَتُهُ ضَرُورِيَّةً مِثْلَ لُزُومِ اجْتِمَاعِ النَّقِيضَيْنِ أَوِ ارْتِفَاعِهِمَا مَعًا وَسَلْبِ الشَّيْءِ عَنْ نَفْسِهِ وَتَقَدُّمِ الشَّيْءِ عَلَى نَفْسِهِ وَخِلَافِ الْمَفْرُوضِ وَأَعْظَمِيَّةِ الْجُزْءِ عَلَى الْكُلِّ وَالدَّوْرِ وَالتَّسَلْسُلِ وَغَيْرِ ذَلِكَ مِنَ الضَّرُورِيَّاتِ أَوْ تَكُونُ بِمَنْزِلَةِ الضَّرُورِيَّاتِ؛ لِكَوْنِهَا مُسَلَّمَةً عِنْدَ الْجُمْهُورِ، كَلُزُومِ ارْتِكَابِ الْمَجَازِ بِلَا قَرِينَةٍ أَوْ عَلَاقَةٍ مُعْتَبَرَةٍ أَوِ الْإِضْمَارِ قَبْلَ الذِّكْرِ لَفْظًا وَرُتْبَةً أَوْ غَيْرِهَا مِنَ الْمُسَلَّمَاتِ عِنْدَ أَهْلِ الْعَرَبِيَّةِ. وَإِنَّمَا وَجَبَ أَدَاءُ حَقِّهِ الْمَذْكُورِ مِنْ كَوْنِ تِلْكَ الْمُقَدِّمَةِ ضَرُورِيَّةً أَوْ بِمَنْزِلَتِهَا لِيَظْهَرَ الْحَقُّ وَيَنْقَطِعَ الْكَلَامُ.

وَإِذِ انْتَهَى هُنَا الْكَلَامُ إِلَى هَذَا الْمَقَامِ، فَنَشْرَعُ فِي الْمَقْصِدِ وَالْمَرَامِ، مُسْتَعِينًا مِنَ اللهِ الْمَلِكِ الْعَلَّامِ.

Section One

THE GENERAL ETIQUETTES FOR ALL TYPES OF RESEARCHERS AND STUDENTS

Every student should begin by mentioning the name of Allah and praising Him ﷻ. Then one should send their sincere salutations upon the Prophet Muhammad ﷺ, and recite the following:

سُبْحَانَكَ لَا عِلْمَ لَنَا إِلَّا مَا عَلَّمْتَنَا إِنَّكَ أَنْتَ الْعَلِيمُ الْحَكِيمُ

"Exalted are You; we have no knowledge except what You have taught us. Indeed, it is You who is the Knowing, the Wise." (2:32)

The verse should be read to the end. Furthermore, one should recite whatever they have memorised from the narrated supplications so that they will gain blessings and enlightenment. One should also face towards the *Qiblah*, which is a place of bounty, and they should humble themselves before Allah ﷻ, asking Him to bestow upon them the truth, inspire them to what is correct, to help them, facilitate for them that which they are seeking, and to make it easy for them.

Thereafter, when beginning a book in any field, the student should attempt to form a mental image of the science. This can be done by studying the common definition of that science. They should also understand the purpose and final goal of the book, and the objective of the topic so that he or she increases in their desire for gaining it, even if they are not a beginner in this field. This is applicable to anyone in pursuit of any knowledge and should be done even if they are not a novice in the science.

Thereafter, the student should conceptualise the topic by focusing on its introductory aspects and its intent or purpose. This conceptualisation is to be done by everyone who is aware

الْمَقْصَدُ الْأَوَّلُ

فِي بَيَانِ الْآدَابِ الْعَامَّةِ إِلَى جَمِيعِ أَنْوَاعِ الْمُطَالِعِينَ

يَجِبُ عَلَى كُلِّ مُطَالِعٍ إِذَا أَرَادَ الشُّرُوعَ فِي الْمُطَالَعَةِ أَنْ يَذْكُرَ اللهَ تَعَالَى، وَيَحْمَدَهُ، وَأَنْ يُصَلِّيَ عَلَى النَّبِيِّ ﷺ، وَأَنْ يَقْرَأَ ﴿سُبْحَانَكَ لَا عِلْمَ لَنَآ إِلَّا مَا عَلَّمْتَنَآ﴾ الْآيَةَ. [البقرة، ٣٢/٢] وَأَنْ يَقْرَأَ مَا فِي حِفْظِهِ مِنَ الْأَدْعِيَةِ الْمَأْثُورَةِ الْوَارِدَةِ فِي طَلَبِ الْفَيْضِ وَإِلْهَامِ الصَّوَابِ، وَأَنْ يَتَوَجَّهَ بِقَلْبِهِ إِلَى جَنَابِ الْفَيَّاضِ الْمُطْلَقِ وَيَتَضَرَّعَ إِلَيْهِ سَائِلًا مِنْهُ إِفَاضَةَ الْحَقِّ وَإِلْهَامَ الصَّوَابِ وَإِعَانَتَهُ عَلَى تَسْهِيلِ الْمَطْلَبِ وَتَيْسِيرِهِ.

ثُمَّ إِنْ كَانَ شَارِعًا فِي كِتَابٍ مِنْ فَنٍّ فَيَنْبَغِي لَهُ أَنْ يَتَصَوَّرَ ذَلِكَ الْفَنَّ بِتَعْرِيفِهِ الْمَأْخُوذِ مِنْ إِحْدَى جِهَتَيْهِ لِيَحْصُلَ لَهُ عِلْمٌ إِجْمَالِيٌّ بِذَلِكَ الْفَنِّ. وَيَتَصَوَّرَ مَوْضُوعَهُ أَيْضًا لِيَتَمَيَّزَ الْمَقْصُودُ عَنْ غَيْرِهِ تَمَيُّزًا مَا، وَيَتَصَوَّرَ غَايَتَهُ وَالْغَرَضَ مِنْهُ لِيَزْدَادَ شَوْقًا إِلَى تَحْصِيلِهِ.

وَإِنْ لَمْ يَكُنْ مُبْتَدِئًا بِهِ بَلْ مُطَالِعًا فِي مَحَلٍّ مَا مِنْ مَبَاحِثِ كِتَابٍ وَجَبَ عَلَيْهِ أَنْ يَتَصَوَّرَ الْمَبْحَثَ إِجْمَالًا فِي أَيِّ شَيْءٍ هُوَ مِنْ

of the methods of study. A student must be aware of what it is he or she is intending to study. The lowest level of those capable of studying are those who wish to gain a practical or applicable knowledge for which they have prepared themselves; those that have learnt the introductory aspects. That preparedness is gained through the conceptualisation of the entire science.

For example, the one who wishes to study or research the topic of the "Existence of Primordial Matter" to understand its reality and to explain it must know and understand that, according to the philosophers, there is something called primordial matter. The philosophers claim that it is a substance and that it exists independently. They further state that it has a body and there are other atoms and substances in it called physical form. This is considered general knowledge, which will create a desire to know the deeper reality of it and solidify that knowledge in depth and detail. One must then go back to sources that will contain the definitions and explanations from the books of philosophy. By doing so, one gains a general understanding of the topic. Seeking these definitions of primordial matter from its sources will give the student the preparedness necessary to proceed in its study.

Then one can begin to study the actual topic in detail. One should start by correcting their pronunciation of the text ('ibārah) and cultivate a good understanding of the text by progressively studying the individual words and sentence structures. Through studying the individual words from the aspect of its root words and their lexical meanings, one will increase their knowledge of lexicology. In so doing, one will be protected from making mistakes from a lexicological perspective. One will also begin to notice similarities and differences between lexical meanings and terminological meanings. Knowing and recognising these similarities will produce other unanticipated benefits. The tendencies to notice similarities will, of course, be according to one's intellectual strength or weakness as well as

الْمَبَادِئِ أَوِ الْمَقَاصِدِ، وَمَا الْمَقْصُودُ مِنْ ذَلِكَ الْمَبْحَثِ مِنْ مَبْدَئِهِ إِلَى مَقْطَعِهِ؛ لِأَنَّ كُلَّ مَبْحَثٍ يُطَالِعُ فِيهِ مَنْ لَهُ نَصِيبٌ مِنَ الْمُطَالَعَةِ، يَجِبُ أَنْ يَكُونَ مَشْعُورًا بِهِ عِنْدَ الْمُطَالِعِ، وَأَنَّ أَدْنَى مَرَاتِبِ الْمُطَالِعِينَ هُوَ الَّذِي يُطَالِعُ الْمَحَلَّ لِتَحْصِيلِ الْعِلْمِ بِالْفِعْلِ وَلَهُ اسْتِعْدَادٌ قَرِيبٌ بِالنِّسْبَةِ إِلَى ذَلِكَ الْمَحَلِّ لَا مَحَالَةَ. وَذَلِكَ الِاسْتِعْدَادُ يَقْتَضِي الشُّعُورَ بِهِ ضَرُورَةً، مِثْلُ مَنْ يُرِيدُ الْمُطَالَعَةَ فِي مَبْحَثِ إِثْبَاتِ الْهَيُولَى لِيَحْصُلَ الْعِلْمُ بِحَقِيقَتِهَا وَإِنِّيَّتِهَا، وَهُوَ يَعْرِفُ لَا مَحَالَةَ أَنَّ عِنْدَ الْحُكَمَاءِ شَيْئًا يُقَالُ لَهُ «الْهَيُولَى»، وَأَنَّهُمْ يَدَّعُونَ جَوْهَرِيَّتَهَا وَثُبُوتَهَا فِي الْخَارِجِ وَتَرَكُّبَ الْجِسْمِ مِنْهَا وَمِنْ جَوْهَرٍ آخَرَ حَالٌّ فِيهَا يُقَالُ لَهُ: «الصُّورَةُ الْجِسْمِيَّةُ». وَبِهَذَا الْعِلْمِ الْإِجْمَالِيِّ حَصَلَ لَهُ شَوْقٌ إِلَى مَعْرِفَةِ حَقِيقَتِهَا وَثُبُوتِهَا تَحْقِيقًا وَتَفْصِيلًا، فَرَجَعَ إِلَى الْمَحَلِّ الْمُتَكَفِّلِ بِتَعْرِيفِهَا وَبَيَانِهَا مِنْ كُتُبِ الْحِكْمَةِ، فَبِذَلِكَ يَقْدِرُ عَلَى التَّصَوُّرِ الْإِجْمَالِيِّ بِأَنَّ الْمَطْلُوبَ مِنَ الْمَحَلِّ مَعْرِفَةُ حَقِيقَةِ الْهَيُولَى وَثُبُوتُهَا تَفْصِيلًا وَتَحْقِيقًا.

ثُمَّ يَشْرَعُ فِي مُلَاحَظَةِ الْمَبْحَثِ تَفْصِيلًا، وَيَبْتَدِئُ بِتَصْحِيحِ الْعِبَارَةِ وَتَهْذِيبِهَا بِمُلَاحَظَةِ مُفْرَدَاتِهَا وَمُرَكَّبَاتِهَا شَيْئًا فَشَيْئًا لِيَحْصُلَ لَهُ بِمُلَاحَظَةِ الْمُفْرَدَاتِ مِنْ جِهَةِ مَوَادِّهَا وَمَعَانِيهَا اللُّغَوِيَّةِ مَلَكَةٌ فِي عِلْمِ اللُّغَةِ، وَيَأْمَنُ بِهَا عَنِ الْغَلَطِ وَالْخَبَطِ مِنْ جِهَةِ اللُّغَةِ، وَتَظْهَرُ لَهُ الْمُنَاسَبَاتُ وَوُجُوهُ الْمُنَاسَبَاتِ بَيْنَ الْمَعَانِي اللُّغَوِيَّةِ وَالِاصْطِلَاحِيَّةِ، وَعَسَى أَنْ يَتَوَلَّدَ مِنْ مَعْرِفَةِ تِلْكَ الْمُنَاسَبَاتِ فَوَائِدُ غَيْرُ مَأْمُولَةٍ بِمَنْزِلَةِ النِّعَمِ الْغَيْرِ الْمُتَرَقَّبَةِ بِحَسَبِ مَرَاتِبِ قُوَّةِ الذِّهْنِ وَصَفَائِهِ وَاسْتِعْدَادِ النَّفْسِ فِي اسْتِخْرَاجِ الْمَطَالِبِ بَعْضِهَا عَنْ بَعْضٍ.

one's readiness to extrapolate meanings from other things. By studying the individual words from the aspects of its form, one masters etymology and will be protected from making mistakes, such as mixing up the forms of different words, which is prevalent among students. The student will be able to differentiate between words in their original state and derived words, and that which is or is not a lexical analogy. Knowing the root letters gives one the ability to differentiate between that which is in its original form, and that which is not.

Perhaps by looking at the additional letters, a student may derive a subtle yet suitable meaning, and thus grow and strengthen his or her capability within the field. Otherwise, if considered alone, the science of etymology is of great benefit, especially for protecting one from mistakes. This is gained by studying individual words from the perspective of their meanings, and differentiating between the root words and the derived words, the general meanings from the specific meanings, the equivocal from unequivocal, lexical meanings from terminologies, and the figurative meanings from the literal meanings. Adhering to this method will give one a proficiency in the science of positing (*'ilm al-waḍ'*), which is the base of all sciences connected to sentence structure. If one were to spend all of their time verifying the coinage of words and letters so as to know the types of words and all three forms, then so be it.

After recognising the set meaning of word forms, one must apply those rules to every word, taking into consideration the specific rulings connected to that type of word form, thus opening up the doors of study and investigation into the intricacies of the Arabic language. Thereafter, the student should begin an investigation of the sentences, their constituent parts, and how these parts are joined together. This study should be based on the rulings of grammar (*naḥw*), looking at the state of each of the words and expressions, and the *i'rāb* that goes appropriately with those words. This type of analysis will grant a keen

وَتَحْصُلُ لَهُ بِمُلَاحَظَةِ الْمُفْرَدَاتِ مِنْ جِهَةِ صُوَرِهَا وَصِيَغِهَا عَلَى مُقْتَضَى أُصُولِ التَّصْرِيفِ مَلَكَةٌ فِي عِلْمِ الصَّرْفِ، وَيَأْمَنُ مِنَ الْغَلَطِ مِنْ جِهَةِ الِاشْتِبَاهِ وَالِالْتِبَاسِ بَيْنَ صُوَرِ الْكَلِمَاتِ فَإِنَّهُ كَثِيرُ الْوُقُوعِ، وَيُمَيِّزُ الْفُرُوعَ عَنِ الْأُصُولِ وَالْمَعْنَى بِالْقِيَاسِ عَنْ غَيْرِهِ وَعَنِ الْبَاقِي عَلَى أَصْلِهِ، فَتَتَمَيَّزُ بِذَلِكَ عِنْدَهُ الْحُرُوفُ الْأَصْلِيَّةُ عَنِ الزَّائِدَةِ، فَعَسَى أَنْ يَسْتَخْرِجَ مِنَ الزَّائِدَةِ مَعَانِيَ دَقِيقَةً مُنَاسِبَةً لِلْمَقَامِ فَيَنْمُو عِلْمُهُ أَوْ يَتَقَوَّى إِنْ كَانَ مِنَ الْمُسْتَعِدِّينَ لِذَلِكَ، وَإِلَّا فَمَلَكَةُ التَّصْرِيفِ فَائِدَةٌ عَظِيمَةٌ فِي حَقِّهِ سِيَّمَا مَعَ الْأَمْنِ مِنَ الْغَلَطِ.

وَيَحْصُلُ لَهُ بِمُلَاحَظَةِ الْمُفْرَدَاتِ مِنْ جِهَةِ وَضْعِهَا لِمَعَانِيهَا تَمْيِيزُ الْكُلِّيِّ عَنِ الْجُزْئِيِّ، وَالْعَامِ عَنِ الْخَاصِّ، وَالْمُفْرَدِ عَنِ الْمُشْتَرَكِ، وَاللُّغَةِ عَنِ الِاصْطِلَاحِ، وَالْحَقِيقَةِ عَنِ الْمَجَازِ. وَبِذَلِكَ تَحْصُلُ مَلَكَةٌ فِي عِلْمِ الْوَضْعِ الَّذِي هُوَ أَسَاسُ الْعُلُومِ الْمُتَعَلِّقَةِ بِالْعِبَارَةِ وَالْأَلْفَاظِ، فَإِنْ كَانَ يَصْرِفُ هِمَّتَهُ فِي تَحْقِيقِ وَضْعِ الْكَلِمَاتِ وَالْأَلْفَاظِ حَتَّى يَعْرِفَ الْوَضْعَ النَّوْعِيَّ بِجَمِيعِ أَنْوَاعِهِ الثَّلَاثَةِ وَالشَّخْصِيِّ كَذَلِكَ، ثُمَّ يَتَأَمَّلَ تَطْبِيقَ وَضْعِ كُلِّ كَلِمَةٍ عَلَى نَوْعٍ مِنْ تِلْكَ الْأَنْوَاعِ، وَيَتَصَوَّرَ الْأَحْكَامَ الْمُخْتَصَّةَ بِذَلِكَ النَّوْعِ مِنَ الْوَضْعِ انْفَتَحَ عَلَيْهِ أَبْوَابُ الدَّقَائِقِ وَالْحَقَائِقِ.

ثُمَّ يَتَصَوَّرُ الْمُرَكَّبَاتِ مِنْ حَيْثُ هِيَ مُرَكَّبَاتٌ وَأَجْزَائِهَا مِنْ حَيْثُ هِيَ أَجْزَاءُ الْمُرَكَّبَاتِ وَمَا يَتَرَتَّبُ عَلَيْهَا مِنَ الْأَحْكَامِ النَّحْوِيَّةِ وَالْأَحْوَالِ الْإِعْرَابِيَّةِ الْمُنَاسِبَةِ لِلْمَقَامِ لِتَحْصُلَ لَهُ مَلَكَةٌ فِي عِلْمِ النَّحْوِ أَيُّ مَلَكَةٍ، وَيَنْحَلُّ

perception of the science of Arabic grammar and an ability to avoid confusion when coming across difficult areas in sentence composition and organisation. Normally, this happens to the one who has not mastered the science of grammar, or one who is absent-minded, not taking into consideration the principles of grammar.

Through this type of study, the student will uncover the various subtleties regarding the intended meanings of phrases and individual words. After determining these meanings, the student can then progress to a deep study of the actual subject matter they are considering. He or she can now explore and roam through the fields of research if they are amongst its great horsemen. Even if they are not from amongst those people, what benefit can there be above foundational knowledge of grammar?

Thereafter, one must study the rhetorical qualities of the words of the text. Different circumstances require an eloquent communicator to consider the most appropriate expressions needed to produce an intended meaning. This eloquence is often achieved by adjusting the word sequence or alternating between specific and non-specific words. Of course, it is necessary for the work itself to be written eloquently in the first place so that the subtleties of meaning are clearly elucidated and easily understood by the expert. These are some factors that masters of rhetoric might take into account, and have established these principles as the central point of rhetoric.

Extended study from this perspective will give one a mastery of ʿilm al-maʿānī, or the science of meanings. One will gain an appreciation for eloquence in speech and rhetoric, which will improve one's understanding of the subtleties of Qur'anic exegesis and the reality of the Qur'an. By this type of study, one also learns the method of understanding complicated meanings. These types of difficult meanings are called by the scholars of interpretation, "desired or sought-after meanings".

لَهُ التَّعْقِيدُ النَّاشِئُ مِنْ سُوءِ التَّأْلِيفِ، وَيَأْمَنُ الْغَلَطَ مِنْ جِهَةِ التَّرْكِيبِ وَهُوَ كَثِيرُ الْوُقُوعِ، وَيَقَعُ فِيهِ غَالِبًا مَنْ لَيْسَ لَهُ مَلَكَةٌ فِي عِلْمِ النَّحْوِ أَوْ يُهْمِلُ مُرَاعَاةَ أُصُولِهِ، وَيَنْكَشِفُ لَهُ وُجُوهُ الْمَزَايَا وَالنِّكَاتِ مِنَ الْمَعَانِي التَّرْكِيبِيَّةِ الزَّائِدَةِ عَلَى مَعَانِي الْمُفْرَدَاتِ. وَبَعْدَ انْكِشَافِ تِلْكَ الْمَعَانِي إِنْ شَاءَ سَلَكَ مِنْ جِهَاتِهَا إِلَى الْمَبَاحِثِ الدَّقِيقَةِ، وَيَجُولُ فِي مِضْمَارِ التَّحْقِيقِ إِنْ كَانَ مِنْ رِجَالِهِ وَفُرْسَانِهِ، وَإِنْ لَمْ يَكُنْ مِنْهُمْ، فَأَيُّ فَائِدَةٍ تُطْلَبُ فَوْقَ فَائِدَةِ حُصُولِ الْمَلَكَةِ النَّحْوِيَّةِ.

ثُمَّ يُلَاحِظُ الْعِبَارَةَ مِنْ جِهَةِ الْخُصُوصِيَّاتِ الَّتِي بِهَا يُطَابِقُ الْكَلَامُ مُقْتَضَى الْحَالِ ظَاهِرَهَا وَبَاطِنَهَا وَهِيَ الْحَالَاتُ الَّتِي تَقْتَضِيهَا طَبَائِعُ الْمَعَانِي مِنْ حَيْثُ هِيَ مَعَانٍ مِنْ تَرْتِيبِهَا بِالتَّقْدِيمِ وَالتَّأْخِيرِ وَتَوْصِيفِهَا بِالتَّعْرِيفِ وَالتَّنْكِيرِ. فَيَجِبُ أَنْ تَكُونَ الْأَلْفَاظُ الدَّالَّةُ عَلَيْهَا أَيْضًا عَلَى ذَلِكَ الْمِنْوَالِ وَالتَّرْتِيبِ حَتَّى تَنْكَشِفَ وُجُوهُ الْمَعَانِي وَتُؤْخَذَ مِنْهَا بِسُهُولَةٍ وَلِذَا اعْتَبَرَهَا الْبُلَغَاءُ وَجَعَلُوهَا مَدَارَ الْبَلَاغَةِ. وَبِهَذِهِ الْمُلَاحَظَةِ تَحْصُلُ مَلَكَةُ عِلْمِ الْمَعَانِي وَذَائِقَةُ الْفَصَاحَةِ وَالْبَلَاغَةِ. فَنِعْمَ الْمَدَارُ وَالْوَسِيلَةُ إِلَى مَعْرِفَةِ دَقَائِقِ التَّفْسِيرِ وَحَقَائِقِ الْقُرْآنِ الْعَظِيمِ. وَبِهَذِهِ الْمُلَاحَظَةِ أَيْضًا يُعْرَفُ طَرِيقُ صَيْدِ الْمَعَانِي الْوُحْشِيَّةِ الْعَرَضِيَّةِ اللَّازِمَةِ مِنَ الْمَعَانِي الْمَأْنُوسَةِ الْوَسَطِيَّةِ، وَيُقَالُ لِتِلْكَ الْمَعَانِي فِي عُرْفِ أَصْحَابِ الْمَعَانِي «الْمَعَانِي الْمُتَصَيَّدَةُ»، وَمَنْ لَمْ يَأْلَفْ بِذَلِكَ وَأَهْمَلَ جَانِبَهُ لَا يَعْرِفُ مُنَاسَبَةَ الْكَلَامِ لَا لِلْحَالِ وَالرِّجَالِ وَلَا لِلْمَقَامِ وَلَا لِلْمَرَامِ، فَلَا يَقْدِرُ عَلَى تَخْرِيجِ الْمَعَانِي الدَّقِيقَةِ الْمُرَتَّبَةِ عَلَى هَذِهِ الْمُنَاسَبَاتِ.

In contrast, the one who does not become familiar with this science and skill will remain uncertain as to the best structure of words for achieving a particular objective. They will not have the ability to adequately express deeper meanings and feelings.

Thereafter, one must review the written work to find if there are any subtleties of *ilm al-bayān*, the science of expression. Such subtleties necessitate certain meanings or imply others, and include similes, parables, figurative speech, metaphorical speech, metonymy, or indirect expressions. In summary, one should look for any type of figurative speech in the written work. Extended study from this perspective will grant mastery over the science of expression, and this is the most important science for recognising the miraculous nature of the Qur'an. One who does this will be gifted with an ability to recognise the subtleties of expressions and the subtleties of necessary and implied meanings written by the masters of rhetoric.

Taking note of the necessary and implied meanings of speech, along with what can be learnt from those meanings, individual words and phrases, root words, derived words, and corresponding words, the student then moves on to looking for secondary intelligible meanings. This refers to those meanings which are understood after the primary meanings have been comprehended. This is the subject matter of logic, which uses the known as a means to reach the unknown. One will look at definitions first to see what type of speech they are, which include verbal, literal, nominal, complete terms, or deficient descriptions. Thereafter, one will analyse all of the parts of the definition to separate between the genus and the specific difference, and also separate between common accidents and particular accidents. The categories of things that can be known are based on the definitions of things.

One must study the various methods for dividing and categorising through meanings and definitions. For example, universal terms can be sub-divided into their constituent parts,

ثُمَّ يُلَاحِظُ الْعِبَارَةَ بِأَنَّهَا هَلْ فِيهَا شَيْءٌ مِنْ لَطَائِفِ عِلْمِ الْبَيَانِ مِمَّا تَتَفَاوَتُ بِهِ وُجُوهُ دَلَالَاتِ الْكَلَامِ عَلَى مَعَانِيهَا الِالْتِزَامِيَّةِ وَالتَّضَمُّنِيَّةِ فِي مَرَاتِبِ الْوُضُوحِ؛ أَعْنِي هَلْ فِيهَا شَيْءٌ مِنَ التَّشْبِيهَاتِ وَالِاسْتِعَارَاتِ وَالْكِنَايَاتِ وَمِنْ سَائِرِ أَقْسَامِ الْمَجَازِ. وَبِالْمُوَاظَبَةِ عَلَى هَذِهِ الْمُلَاحَظَةِ تَحْصُلُ مَلَكَةُ عِلْمِ الْبَيَانِ، وَهِيَ أَعْظَمُ الْوَسَائِلِ إِلَى مَعْرِفَةِ إِعْجَازِ الْقُرْآنِ. وَبِتِلْكَ الْمُلَاحَظَةِ يَظْفَرُ بِدَقَائِقِ عِبَارَاتِ الْفُصَحَاءِ وَالْبُلَغَاءِ وَبِدَقَائِقِ مَعَانِيهَا اللُّزُومِيَّةِ وَالضِّمْنِيَّةِ.

وَبَعْدَ إِتْمَامِ مُلَاحَظَةِ الْعِبَارَةِ وَمَا يُسْتَفَادُ مِنْهَا مِنَ الْمَعَانِي الْإِفْرَادِيَّةِ وَالتَّرْكِيبِيَّةِ وَالْأَصْلِيَّةِ وَالْفَرْعِيَّةِ وَالْمُطَابِقِيَّةِ وَالتَّضَمُّنِيَّةِ وَالِالْتِزَامِيَّةِ، يَنْبَغِي لَهُ أَنْ يُلَاحِظَ الْمَحَلَّ بِالْمَعْقُولَاتِ الثَّانِيَةِ أَيْضًا؛ أَيِ الْحَالَاتِ الَّتِي تَتَعَقَّلُ فِي الْمَرْتَبَةِ الثَّانِيَةِ، وَهِيَ الَّتِي يُبْحَثُ عَنْهَا فِي عِلْمِ الْمَنْطِقِ، وَهِيَ تَعْرِضُ لِلْمَعْقُولَاتِ الْأُولَى مِنْ حَيْثُ أَنَّهَا مُوَصِّلَةٌ إِلَى الْمَجْهُولَاتِ.

فَيُلَاحِظُ التَّعْرِيفَاتِ أَوَّلًا بِأَنَّهَا مِنْ أَيِّ قِسْمٍ مِنْ أَقْسَامِ الْقَوْلِ الشَّارِحِ هَلْ هُوَ لَفْظِيٌّ أَوِ اسْمِيٌّ أَوْ حَقِيقِيٌّ، وَهَلْ هُوَ حَدٌّ تَامٌّ أَوْ نَاقِصٌ أَوْ رَسْمٌ تَامٌّ أَوْ نَاقِصٌ، ثُمَّ يُلَاحِظُ أَجْزَاءَ كُلِّ تَعْرِيفٍ فَيُمَيِّزُ الْجِنْسَ عَنِ الْفَصْلِ وَالْعَرْضَ الْعَامَّ عَنِ الْخَاصِّ وَالْمُفَارِقَ عَنِ اللَّازِمِ. وَأَمَّا التَّقْسِيمَاتُ فَهِيَ رَاجِعَةٌ فِي الْحَقِيقَةِ إِلَى التَّعْرِيفَاتِ؛ فَيُلَاحِظُ فِيهَا هَلْ هِيَ مِنْ قَبِيلِ

in which the whole universal term does not apply to each individual part of the category. Alternatively, universal terms can be defined by subclasses. In the latter division, the universal concept can be applied to each and every one of the individuals of the group. The difference between these two categories is that the first divides the whole into parts which, taken together, form the whole. In the second division however, the universals are broken down according to its different individual members. Then, one must look at whether these definitions are restrictive or non-restrictive, and whether the restriction, if present, is a complete restriction or mere inductive reasoning.

Thereafter, one should also study all the propositions and determine which type of proposition it is. Is it a singular or a compound word? Is it a real proposition, a conceptual composition, or an existent proposition in reality? Is it attributive or conditional? If it is conditional, is it conjunctive or disjunctive? If it is conjunctive, is it mandatorily conjunctive, coincidentally conjunctive, or a true disjunctive proposition, non-combining, or simply devoid? One will also look to see if it is individual or if it is restrictive. If it is restrictive, is it indeterminate?

In all of these stated categories, one must see if it is a negative or positive statement, and then examine the contradiction of this proposition and the equivalent conversion of it. Lastly, one must differentiate between the claim and the proof. One must begin by looking at the proof: is it a type of syllogism, which is based on proof? Or is it a disputation syllogism? No proofs other than these two types (from the five extant types) are mentioned in recognised sciences, except very rarely. All of these go back to either induction or analogy, or continuation in preceding condition. Anything other than that which we have mentioned gives nothing but speculative knowledge in any area of study.

If one recognises a type of syllogism, then one must look to see if it is true, if it is coupled syllogism, or if it is an excep-

تَقْسِيمِ الْكُلِّ إِلَى الْأَجْزَاءِ وَهُوَ نَادِرٌ فِي الْعُلُومِ أَوْ مِنْ قَبِيلِ تَقْسِيمِ الْكُلِّيِّ إِلَى الْجُزْئِيَّاتِ، وَيُمَيِّزُ بَيْنَهُمَا بِصِحَّةِ حَمْلِ الْمُقَسَّمِ عَلَى كُلِّ وَاحِدٍ مِنَ الْأَقْسَامِ فِي الثَّانِي دُونَ الْأَوَّلِ. ثُمَّ يُلَاحِظُهَا بِأَنَّهَا حَاصِرَةٌ أَوْ غَيْرُ حَاصِرَةٍ وَحَصْرُهَا عَقْلِيٌّ وَاسْتِقْرَائِيٌّ وَيَتَأَمَّلُ فِي وَجْهِ الْحَصْرِ.

ثُمَّ يُلَاحِظُ كُلَّ مُرَكَّبٍ مِنَ الْمُرَكَّبَاتِ الْكَلَامِيَّةِ وَالْإِخْبَارِيَّةِ بِأَنَّهُ مِنْ أَيِّ قِسْمٍ مِنْ أَقْسَامِ الْقَضَايَا، هَلْ هِيَ بَسِيطَةٌ أَوْ مُرَكَّبَةٌ، وَهَلْ هِيَ حَقِيقَةٌ أَوْ ذِهْنِيَّةٌ أَوْ خَارِجِيَّةٌ، وَهَلْ هِيَ حَمْلِيَّةٌ أَوْ شَرْطِيَّةٌ، وَهَلِ الشَّرْطِيَّةُ مُتَّصِلَةٌ أَوْ مُنْفَصِلَةٌ، وَهَلِ الْمُتَّصِلَةُ لُزُومِيَّةٌ أَوِ اتِّفَاقِيَّةٌ، وَهَلِ الْمُنْفَصِلَةُ حَقِيقِيَّةٌ أَوْ مَانِعَةُ الْجَمْعِ فَقَطْ أَوْ مَانِعَةُ الْخُلُوِّ فَقَطْ، وَهَلْ هِيَ شَخْصِيَّةٌ أَوْ مَحْصُورَةٌ، وَهَلِ الْمَحْصُورَةُ مُسَوَّرَةٌ أَوْ مُهْمَلَةٌ، وَهَلِ الْمُسَوَّرَةُ كُلِّيَّةٌ أَوْ جُزْئِيَّةٌ، وَهَلْ هِيَ مُوَجَّهَةٌ أَوْ مُطْلَقَةٌ، وَأَنَّ كُلَّ وَاحِدٍ مِنْ هَذِهِ الْأَقْسَامِ هَلْ هِيَ مُوجَبَةٌ أَوْ سَالِبَةٌ، ثُمَّ يُلَاحِظُ نَقِيضَهَا وَعَكْسَهَا الْمُسْتَوِي وَالنَّقِيضَ.

ثُمَّ يُمَيِّزُ الدَّعْوَى عَنِ الدَّلِيلِ فَيَشْرَعُ فِي مُلَاحَظَةِ الدَّلِيلِ هَلْ هُوَ مِنْ بَابِ الْقِيَاسِ الْبُرْهَانِيِّ أَوِ الْخَطَابِيِّ أَوِ الْجَدَلِيِّ؛ لِأَنَّ مَاعَدَا هَذِهِ الثَّلَاثَةِ مِنَ الصِّنَاعَاتِ الْخَمْسِ لَا يُذْكَرُ فِي الْعُلُومِ الْمُعْتَبَرَةِ إِلَّا نَادِرًا أَوْ هُوَ مِنْ قَبِيلِ الِاسْتِقْرَاءِ أَوِ التَّمْثِيلِ أَوِ الِاسْتِحْسَانِ أَوِ اسْتِصْحَابِ الْحَالِ أَوْ غَيْرِهَا مِمَّا يُفِيدُ الظَّنَّ عَلَى مَا يَتَحَمَّلُهُ الْفَنُّ.

tion. They must also look to see phrases which logically lead to the result. Thereafter, one must look at which of the forms they must take, consider the conditions of each of the forms, and determine if everything is present. Then they must see if the syllogism is complete, having all of its premises connected together. If it is incomplete by having only one premise (the major or the minor), one should question if this is due to the extreme clarity of the other premise or not. Sometimes, the proof is mentioned only as a kind of warning. If this is the case, one must look at the conclusion of the discussions to find out if it is a necessary conclusion. There may be a level of leniency in acceptance of the proofs. If one continuously persists in studying from this perspective, they will attain a great benefit: the mastery and excellence in the science of logic. It is a mastery by which correct thinking is differentiated from incorrect thinking, and the best is differentiated from the worst.

And how could this not be the case, when the science of logic is the benchmark of intellect? The one who does not test their opinions and thoughts according to this scale will possess incorrect analogies and syllogism, and they will be in loss. The one who does not sharpen their intellect and cultivate their mind with logic, their thoughts and opinions will be full of mistakes. Logic is that which sets thinking straight, just as grammar sets the tongue straight. The truth is that these two noble sciences are two doorways for every student in reaching their perfection. Thus, it is necessary for every student to strive and exert themselves fully to gain these two faculties and all that they contain, thus allowing them to utilise these in all of their studies and research.

One should not pay attention to statements that say "logic leads to misguidance". Rather, one should understand that this is mere ignorance and a type of blind following. Imam al-Ghazālī 🙵, has stated in some of his works regarding the mandatory nature of learning logic for every person of intel-

وَإِذَا تَعَيَّنَ كَوْنُهُ قِيَاسًا يُلَاحَظُ أَوَّلًا أَنَّهُ مُسْتَقِيمٌ أَوْ خَلَفٌ اقْتِرَانِيٌّ أَوِ اسْتِثْنَائِيٌّ مُفْرَدٌ أَوْ مُرَكَّبٌ مَوْصُولُ النَّتَائِجِ أَوْ مَفْصُولُهَا. ثُمَّ يُلَاحَظُ أَنَّهُ مِنْ أَيِّ شَكْلٍ هُوَ مِنَ الْأَشْكَالِ الْأَرْبَعَةِ، وَمِنْ أَيِّ ضَرْبٍ مِنْ ضُرُوبِ ذَلِكَ الشَّكْلِ، وَيُلَاحَظُ شُرُوطُ الشَّكْلِ وَالضَّرْبِ بِأَنَّهَا مَوْجُودَةٌ أَوْ مَفْقُودَةٌ، ثُمَّ يُلَاحَظُ أَنَّهُ تَامٌّ قَدْ ذَكَرَ جَمِيعَ مُقَدِّمَاتِهِ مُرَتَّبَةً أَوْ غَيْرَ مُرَتَّبَةٍ أَوْ نَاقِصٌ قَدِ اقْتُصِرَ إِمَّا عَلَى ذِكْرِ الْكُبْرَى لِكَوْنِ الصُّغْرَى سَهْلَةَ الْحُصُولِ أَوْ عَلَى الصُّغْرَى لِكَوْنِ الْكُبْرَى ظَاهِرَةً أَوْ مَشْهُورَةً أَوْ عَلَى الْحَدِّ الْأَوْسَطِ فَقَطْ لِكَوْنِ الدَّلِيلِ بِمَنْزِلَةِ التَّنْبِيهِ.

ثُمَّ يُلَاحَظُ مَقْطَعَ الْبَحْثِ بِأَنَّهُ عَلَى حَقِّهِ اللَّازِمِ مِنَ الضَّرُورَةِ أَوِ التَّسْلِيمِ أَوْ لَيْسَ كَذَلِكَ، وَبِالْمُدَاوَمَةِ عَلَى هَذِهِ الْمُلَاحَظَةِ تَحْصُلُ لَهُ فَائِدَةٌ أَيُّ فَائِدَةٍ أَعْنِي مَلَكَةَ عِلْمِ الْمَنْطِقِ، وَهِيَ مَلَكَةٌ بِهَا يَتَمَيَّزُ صَحِيحُ الْفِكْرِ عَنْ فَاسِدِهِ وَرَاجِحُهُ عَنْ كَاسِدِهِ. وَكَيْفَ لَا، وَعِلْمُ الْمَنْطِقِ مِيزَانُ الْعُقُولِ وَالْعُلُومِ، وَمَنْ لَمْ يَزِنْ نَظَرَهُ وَفِكْرَهُ بِهَذَا الْمِيزَانِ لَمْ يُنْتِجْ قِيَاسُهُ سِوَى الْخُسْرَانِ، وَمَنْ لَمْ يُرَوِّضْ ذِهْنَهُ وَلَمْ يُهَذِّبْ عَقْلَهُ بِهِ لَا يَخْلُو فِي أَفْكَارِهِ وَأَنْظَارِهِ عَنِ الْخِذْلَانِ وَهُوَ مُقَوِّمُ الْأَذْهَانِ كَمَا أَنَّ النَّحْوَ مُقَوِّمُ اللِّسَانِ.

وَالْحَقُّ أَنَّ هَذَيْنِ الْعِلْمَيْنِ الشَّرِيفَيْنِ بِمَنْزِلَةِ الْأَبَوَيْنِ لِلطَّالِبِ فِي تَرْبِيَتِهِ وَإِيصَالِهِ إِلَى الْكَمَالِ. فَيَجِبُ عَلَى كُلِّ طَالِبٍ أَنْ يَسْعَى وَيَجِدَّ لِتَحْصِيلِ الْمَلَكَةِ فِيهِمَا بِمُرَاعَاتِهِمَا فِي جَمِيعِ مُطَالَعَاتِهِ وَمُلَاحَظَاتِهِ. وَلَا يُصْغِي إِلَى قَوْلِ مَنْ نَسَبَ تَعَلُّمَ الْمَنْطِقِ إِلَى الضَّلَالِ وَيَحْمِلُ ذَلِكَ عَلَى جَهْلِهِ بِهِ أَوْ عَلَى تَعَصُّبِهِ الْبَارِدِ؛ لِأَنَّ الْإِمَامَ الْغَزَالِيَّ رَضِيَ اللهُ عَنْهُ قَدْ أَثْبَتَ فِي بَعْضِ مُؤَلَّفَاتِهِ وُجُوبَ تَعَلُّمِ الْمَنْطِقِ عَلَى كُلِّ عَاقِلٍ وَهَذَا هُوَ الْإِنْصَافُ.

lect, and this is a balanced statement. After one has studied from this perspective, looking at the words and meanings, and at the first and second set of meanings, then they should make a summary of the topic and all that it covers from beginning to end. This will assist in making their knowledge solid. For example, one should say, "the summary of this section is..." or "the gist of these words are...". For example, "the summary of this work is that it is known what the universe is, and what non-eternal matter is. Then the ruling of non-eternalness is applied to the universe, and this is proven by change. Sometimes this is refuted, and sometimes contradicted. Sometimes these contradictions, objections, and refutations are responded to in such-and-such form."

Thereafter, once the summary has been established in the mind, they must think it over from every perspective and let their mind contemplate it many times so that it becomes firm, and so that they gain a continual benefit from repeated study of the materials.

If it is difficult for someone to make a summary of the topic and to establish it in their mind, it may be due to various reasons:

1. A problem in the verbiage or wording. For example, a lack of clarity in the written work itself makes it difficult for one to specify the intended meaning. It could also be due to a mistake in the writing; a poor compilation of words, incorrect grammar, or without consideration of the subtle meanings of compound statements and words. For example, one may come across a written work whose meaning is impossible to decipher because of a poor compilation from the author, or because of a weak correlation to relatable subject matters, or for other reasons which make it difficult to understand and hard to arrive at the intended meanings. The only way to remove difficulties when the wording is difficult to

وَبَعْدَ إِتْمَامِ هَذِهِ الْمُلَاحَظَاتِ اللَّفْظِيَّةِ وَالْمَعْنَوِيَّةِ وَالْأَوَّلِيَّةِ وَالثَّانَوِيَّةِ يَأْخُذُ خُلَاصَةَ الْمَبْحَثِ وَمَضْمُونَهُ مِنْ مَبْدَئِهِ إِلَى مَقْطَعِهِ، وَيَتَصَوَّرُهُ فِي ذِهْنِهِ وَيُمَكِّنُهُ فِيهِ بِأَنْ يَقُولَ مَثَلًا «حَاصِلُ الْمَبْحَثِ وَخُلَاصَةُ الْكَلَامِ أَنَّهُ قَدْ عَرَّفَ الْعَالَمَ وَالْحُدُوثَ أَوَّلًا، ثُمَّ حَكَمَ عَلَى الْعَالَمِ بِالْحُدُوثِ، وَاسْتَدَلَّ عَلَيْهِ بِالتَّغَيُّرِ، وَمَنَعَ تَارَةً وَنُوقِضَ تَارَةً وَعُورِضَ تَارَةً، ثُمَّ أُجِيبَ عَنِ الْمَنْعِ بِإِثْبَاتِ الْمُقَدِّمَةِ الْمَمْنُوعَةِ أَوْ بِإِبْطَالِ السَّنَدِ الْمُسَاوِي، وَعَنِ النَّقْضِ بِمَنْعِ جَرَيَانِ الدَّلِيلِ فِي مَادَّةِ التَّخَلُّفِ أَوْ بِمَنْعِ التَّخَلُّفِ عَنِ الْمُعَارَضَةِ إِمَّا بِالْمَنْعِ أَوْ بِالنَّقْضِ أَوْ بِالْمُعَارَضَةِ، ثُمَّ رَدَّ الْجَوَابَ بِطَرِيقِ كَذَا وَكَذَا». فَإِذَا قَرَّرَ الْخُلَاصَةَ فِي الذِّهْنِ يَتَأَمَّلُ فِيهِ مِنْ كُلِّ جِهَةٍ، وَيُدِيرُ فِكْرَهُ فِيهِ كَرَّةً بَعْدَ أُخْرَى لِلْإِتْقَانِ وَتَحْصِيلِ الْفَوَائِدِ اللَّازِمَةِ مِنْ تَكْرَارِ النَّظَرِ.

وَإِنْ صَعُبَ عَلَيْهِ أَخْذُ الْخُلَاصَةِ مِنَ الْمَبْحَثِ وَتَقْرِيرُهُ فِي ذِهْنِهِ، فَهَذِهِ الصُّعُوبَةُ لَهَا أَسْبَابٌ كَثِيرَةٌ: مِنْهَا مَا هُوَ لَفْظِيٌّ: مِثْلُ الْقُصُورِ فِي تَهْذِيبِ الْعِبَارَةِ، وَتَحْرِيرِ الْأَلْفَاظِ بِتَعْيِينِ الْمَعَانِي الْمُرَادَةِ مِنْهَا، وَمِثْلُ الْخَطَأِ فِي تَأْلِيفِهَا وَالْإِسَاءَةِ فِي تَرْكِيبِهَا، وَعَدَمِ إِعْطَائِهَا حَقَّهَا مِنْ جِهَةِ النَّحْوِ وَمِنْ جِهَةِ اعْتِبَارِ الْخُصُوصِيَّاتِ الْمُعْتَبَرَةِ فِي الْمُرَكَّبَاتِ، وَمِثْلُ كَوْنِ الْعِبَارَةِ فِي أَصْلِهَا مُعَقَّدَةً بِسَبَبِ سُوءِ التَّأْلِيفِ مِنَ الْمُصَنِّفِ أَوْ بِسَبَبِ ضَعْفِ الْقَرَائِنِ، وَالْعَلَاقَاتِ الِارْتِبَاطِيَّةِ وَغَيْرِ ذَلِكَ مِمَّا يَقْتَضِي عُسْرَ الْفَهْمِ وَضَعْفَ الدَّلَالَةِ. فَطَرِيقُ التَّسْهِيلِ وَإِزَالَةِ الصُّعُوبَةِ فِي هَذَا الْقِسْمِ، أَيْ فِيمَا يَكُونُ سَبَبُ الصُّعُوبَةِ فِيهِ لَفْظِيًّا، أَنْ يُكَرِّرَ النَّظَرَ وَالتَّأَمُّلَ فِي تَهْذِيبِ الْأَلْفَاظِ مِنْ جِهَةِ ذَوَاتِهَا وَمَعَانِيهَا وَمِنْ جِهَةِ تَرْكِيبِهَا وَتَأْلِيفِهَا حَتَّى يَجِدَ فِيهِ مَنْشَأَ الصُّعُوبَةِ وَالْإِشْكَالِ وَيُزِيلَهُ.

understand is to contemplate over the words and try to decipher their meaning by adjusting the words according to their essence and meaning, and according to their compilation, until one finds in themselves clarification for their objections and for their misunderstandings.

2. Another problem may be from the perspective of meaning, for example when the meaning of the entire discussion is particularly subtle, either due to the reader's comprehension or in relation to the work that he or she is reading. The difficulty experienced due to a subtlety in meaning is obvious. However, the difficulty experienced due to uncommonness may not be, so we will explain what this means. Uncommonness is where the intended meaning is not mentioned in books on this topic and is not familiar to specialists in this field, or when it is well-known to a specialist but the reader is not acquainted with it. It may also arise when the reader is acquainted with the concept, but the manner in which it is stated, or the methodology which is used to explain it, is difficult. These types of difficulties are removed by repeatedly going over the text and continuous study.

3. Another example of a difficulty in understanding the meaning is when the discussion is very long and has many branches. This can be due to the fact that the author is proving something through premises which in themselves have individual proofs, and these proofs are connected to one, two, or even three other things. In any of these situations, there are many claims and many proofs. The original statements become compounded with the derived conclusions. The claims and proofs become intermingled with one another, so that one becomes confused due to the overlapping discussions. The reason for this is because the mind is simple. It flees from abundance when it is overwhelmed, especially if

وَمِنْهَا مَا هُوَ مَعْنَوِيٌّ: مِثْلُ أَنْ يَكُونَ الْمَعْنَى الْحَاصِلُ مِنْ مَجْمُوعِ الْبَحْثِ مَعْنًى دَقِيقًا أَوْ غَرِيبًا إِمَّا فِي نَفْسِهِ أَوْ بِالنِّسْبَةِ إِلَى الْمُطَالِعِ. أَمَّا دِقَّتُهُ فَظَاهِرَةٌ، وَأَمَّا غَرَابَتُهُ فَبِأَنْ يَكُونَ ذِكْرُهُ قَلِيلًا فِي الْكُتُبِ بِحَيْثُ لَمْ يَقْرَعْ إِلَّا أَسْمَاعَ الْخَوَاصِّ مِنَ الْعُلَمَاءِ أَوْ بِأَنْ تَكُونَ لَهُ هَذِهِ الْغَرَابَةُ بِالنِّسْبَةِ إِلَى الْمُطَالِعِ، وَإِنْ كَانَتْ فِي نَفْسِهِ مَعْرُوفًا مَأْنُوسًا لِكَثِيرٍ مِنَ الْعُلَمَاءِ بِحَيْثُ لَمْ يَقْرَعْ سَمْعَهُ بِهَذِهِ الصُّورَةِ وَالْأُسْلُوبِ أَصْلًا فَيَزُولُ بِتَكْرَارِ أَخْذِهِ مِنَ الْعِبَارَةِ وَمُلَاحَظَتِهَا بِمُعَاوَنَتِهَا.

وَمِثْلُ أَنْ يَكُونَ الْمَبْحَثُ طَوِيلَ الذَّيْلِ كَثِيرَ الشُّعَبِ؛ إِمَّا بِسَبَبِ أَنْ يَلْتَزِمَ الْمُصَنِّفُ إِثْبَاتَ كُلِّ مُقَدِّمَةٍ نَظَرِيَّةٍ بِدَلِيلٍ مُسْتَقِلٍّ بِمَرْتَبَةٍ أَوْ مَرْتَبَتَيْنِ أَوْ بِمَرَاتِبَ. فَعَلَى كُلِّ تَقْدِيرٍ مِنَ الْمَذْكُورِينَ تَتَكَثَّرُ الدَّعَاوَى وَالْأَدِلَّةُ، وَتَخْتَلِطُ الْأُصُولُ بِالْفُرُوعِ، وَتَتَدَاخَلُ الدَّعَاوَى وَالْأَدِلَّةُ بَعْضُهَا فِي بَعْضٍ فَيَتَشَوَّشُ الذِّهْنُ وَيَضْطَرِبُ النَّظَرُ بِسَبَبِ هَذِهِ الْكَثْرَةِ مَعَ الِاخْتِلَاطِ وَالتَّدَاخُلِ؛ لِأَنَّ الذِّهْنَ بَسِيطٌ يَنْفِرُ مِنَ الْكَثْرَةِ، إِذَا خُلِّيَ وَطَبْعُهُ سِيَّمَا إِذَا كَانَتِ الْكَثْرَةُ مُشَوَّشَةً غَيْرَ مُرَتَّبَةٍ فَإِنَّهُ أَيِ الذِّهْنُ إِنَّمَا يُدْرِكُ الْكَثْرَةَ بَعْدَ أَنْ يَضْبِطَهَا بِجِهَةٍ وَحْدَةٍ يُعِدُّ بِسَبَبِهَا صُورَةً وَحْدَانِيَّةً بِتَرْتِيبِهَا تَرْتِيبًا مُعْتَبَرًا عِنْدَ الْمِيزَانِيِّينَ وَجَعَلَهَا فِي حُكْمِ الْوَاحِدِ الْبَسِيطِ بِذَلِكَ التَّرْتِيبِ الْمَعْقُولِ.

this abundance is confusing and unorganised. Indeed, the mind will only be able to conceive many things after it has solidified it from one perspective and organised everything into one form with a sequence that is understood, and it has put everything into one simple category. In both of these situations, the way of making it easy to understand is to differentiate between the original concepts and that which is derived from the original. Then, they must differentiate between the claims and the proofs, and also from secondary claims and their associated proofs. One must also put them in a natural order, and not look at a deduced branch before one has solidified the original along with its proof. Thereafter, one will go to that which branches off naturally. They must completely ignore the mention of anything if it seems to be out of the natural order. Rather, they should try to obtain a summary and make that summary firm in their mind, just as they did with the original. They must then go to that which naturally follows and do exactly what they did with the first set of information, and do this continually throughout the entire discussion. They should not go to another level until the first level has been solidified and they have separated the claims from the proofs. By levels, we mean categories, the first of which deals with claims and proofs. The second level deals with learning the secondary proofs for the premises of the first proof mentioned to affirm the claim. The third level is learning the proofs for the secondary proof, and so on, until one reaches the necessary conclusion or, at the very least, the accepted conclusion. Regarding the second category, the first stage is looking at the stated proofs for the original claim and its associated claims. The second stage is to look at the associated claims and its proofs, and everything that is on the level of the asso-

وَطُرُقُ التَّسْهِيلِ فِي كُلِّ وَاحِدٍ مِنْ هَذَيْنِ الْقِسْمَيْنِ أَنْ يُمَيِّزَ الْأَصْلَ عَنِ الْفَرْعِ، وَيُمَيِّزَ كُلَّ دَعْوَى مَعَ دَلِيلِهَا عَنْ دَعْوَى أُخْرَى مَعَ دَلِيلِهَا، وَيُرَتِّبَهَا عَلَى التَّرْتِيبِ الطَّبِيعِيِّ، وَلَا يَلْتَفِتُ إِلَى الْفَرْعِ قَبْلَ إِتْقَانِ الْأَصْلِ مَعَ دَلِيلِهِ وَتَقْرِيرِهِ فِي الذِّهْنِ.

ثُمَّ يَنْتَقِلُ إِلَى مَا يَلِيهِ طَبْعًا وَلَا يَلْتَفِتُ إِلَى الْوَضْعِ وَالذِّكْرِ إِنْ كَانَ مُخَالِفًا لِلطَّبْعِ، فَيَأْخُذُهُ خُلَاصَةً وَيُقَرِّرُهُ فِي الذِّهْنِ كَمَا فَعَلَ فِي الْأَصْلِ ثُمَّ إِلَى مَا يَلِيهِ طَبْعًا، وَيَفْعَلُ فِيهِ مَا فَعَلَ فِي الْأَوَّلِ ثُمَّ وَثُمَّ إِلَى آخِرِ الْمَبْحَثِ.

وَأَيْضًا لَا يَنْتَقِلُ مِنْ مَرْتَبَةٍ إِلَى أُخْرَى قَبْلَ تَقْرِيرِ مَا فِي الْأُولَى مِنَ الدَّعَاوَى وَالْأَدِلَّةِ. وَالْمُرَادُ مِنَ الْمَرَاتِبِ إِمَّا فِي الْقِسْمِ الْأَوَّلِ: فَالْمَرْتَبَةُ الْأُولَى: هِيَ الَّتِي تَشْتَمِلُ عَلَى الدَّعْوَى وَدَلِيلِهَا. وَالثَّانِيَةُ: مَا تَشْتَمِلُ عَلَى أَدِلَّةٍ وَمُقَدِّمَاتِ الدَّلِيلِ الْأَوَّلِ الَّتِي أُورِدَتْ فِي إِثْبَاتِهَا. وَالثَّالِثَةُ: مَا تَشْتَمِلُ عَلَى أَدِلَّةِ الْأَدِلَّةِ الثَّانِيَةِ وَهَلُمَّ جَرًّا إِلَى أَنْ يَنْتَهِيَ إِلَى الضَّرُورِيَّاتِ أَوْ إِلَى الْمُسَلَّمَاتِ عِنْدَ الْكُلِّ. هَذَا عَلَى تَقْدِيرِ عَدَمِ تَسْلِيمِ الْخَصْمِ. وَأَمَّا عِنْدَ تَسْلِيمِهِ بِأَيِّ وَجْهٍ كَانَ فَيَنْقَطِعُ فِي الْأُولَى أَوْ فِي الثَّانِيَةِ وَإِنْ لَمْ يَنْتَهِ إِلَى مَا ذُكِرَ.

وَأَمَّا الْقِسْمُ الثَّانِي: فَالْمَرْتَبَةُ الْأُولَى فِيهِ: هِيَ الَّتِي تَشْتَمِلُ عَلَى الْأَنْظَارِ الْمُورَدَةِ عَلَى دَلِيلِ الْأَصْلِ مَعَ أَجْوِبَتِهَا. وَالثَّانِيَةُ: هِيَ الَّتِي تَشْتَمِلُ عَلَى الْأَنْظَارِ الْمُورَدَةِ عَلَى الْأَجْوِبَةِ أَوْ عَلَى مَا فِي مَنْزِلَتِهَا. وَقِسِ الثَّالِثَةَ وَالرَّابِعَةَ عَلَيْهَا.

ciated claims. Thus, one can understand the procedure throughout the entire discussion.

4. Another cause of difficulty when studying is a lack of readiness in the student for extrapolation from that particular topic. A student should be ready for a science before beginning its study.

5. Having an unclear or clouded mind will also make studying difficult. This may be due to a natural quality in the student himself, or due to some external factor such as an onslaught of anxious thoughts, anxieties, or concerns. In this case, one should delay their studies until another time, because having clarity of mind and focus of attention is the fulcrum of any action. It should also be understood that for every time of the day there is a special effect which cannot be found in any other time of the day.

The sign of one being able to summarise the topic well is that the student is able to express the information in different and more concise words than the original statement. For example, one may ask, "What is the gist of this speech?", "What is the summary of this discussion?", or "What is the point?" In response, one may say, "The discussion concerns the topic of affirming a natural form for every natural body, and the proof that comes with that." The student would say, explaining the summary of the claim, "The claim is that natural forms are found for everyone and the summary of the proof is that the commonality found among all things is the existence of finiteness. The first thing that is being affirmed is general form. Thereafter, natural form is being established. The summary of the discussion and the question being asked is the unacceptable nature of the major premise from a secondary proof, and a summary of the reply to this is that the premise, which is refuted, has been established..." and so on and so forth until the end of the entire discussion. The student should continue

وَمِنْ أَسْبَابِ الصُّعُوبَةِ: قُصُورُ اسْتِعْدَادِ الْمُطَالِعِ فِي اسْتِخْرَاجِ ذَلِكَ الْمَبْحَثِ، فَيَسْعَى فِي تَكْمِيلِ الِاسْتِعْدَادِ. وَمِنْهَا أَيْضًا: كُدُورَةُ ذِهْنِهِ إِمَّا بِحَسَبِ الْمِزَاجِ أَوْ بِسَبَبٍ خَارِجِيٍّ مِثْلِ هُجُومِ الْخَوَاطِرِ وَالْهَوَاجِسِ، فَيُؤَخِّرُ الْمُطَالَعَةَ إِلَى وَقْتٍ آخَرَ؛ لِأَنَّ صَفْوَ الذِّهْنِ وَجَمْعِيَّةَ الْخَاطِرِ مَدَارُ الْعَمَلِ. وَأَيْضًا لِكُلِّ وَقْتٍ فَيْضٌ خَاصٌّ لَا يُوجَدُ فِي غَيْرِهِ.

وَأَمَّا أَمَارَةُ أَخْذِ الْخُلَاصَةِ مِنَ الْمَبْحَثِ وَفَهْمِ حَاصِلِ الْكَلَامِ فَهِيَ: أَنْ يَقْتَدِرَ عَلَى التَّعْبِيرِ عَنْهُ بِأَيِّ عِبَارَةٍ شَاءَ وَبِأَوْجَزِ الْعِبَارَاتِ وَأَخْصَرِهَا إِذَا طُولِبَ بِهِ وَسُئِلَ، بِأَنْ يُقَالَ: مَا حَاصِلُ الْكَلَامِ وَفَذْلِكَةُ الْمَبْحَثِ وَخُلَاصَةُ الْمَرَامِ؟ مِثْلَ أَنْ يَكُونَ الْمَبْحَثُ إِثْبَاتَ أَنَّ لِكُلِّ جِسْمٍ طَبِيعِيٍّ شَكْلًا طَبِيعِيًّا مَعَ الدَّلِيلِ الْمُورَدِ عَلَيْهِ، فَتَقُولُ فِي بَيَانِ الْحَاصِلِ: أَنَّ الدَّعْوَى إِثْبَاتُ الشَّكْلِ الطَّبِيعِيِّ لِكُلِّ جِسْمٍ. وَخُلَاصَةُ الدَّلِيلِ: أَنَّ الْحَدَّ الْأَوْسَطَ هُوَ وُجُوبُ التَّنَاهِي وَالثَّابِتُ بِهِ أَوَّلًا مُطْلَقُ الشَّكْلِ ثُمَّ بِهِ الشَّكْلُ الطَّبِيعِيُّ. وَحَاصِلُ الْمَبْحَثِ وَالسُّؤَالِ مَنْعُ الْكُبْرَى مِنْ دَلِيلِ الْمَرْتَبَةِ الثَّانِيَةِ وَحَاصِلُ الْجَوَابِ إِثْبَاتُ الْمُقَدِّمَةِ الْمَمْنُوعَةِ كَذَا وَكَذَا إِلَى مَقْطَعِ الْمَبْحَثِ.

to contemplate over this summary after they have understood it and it has become well-established in their mind.

One should now look over their summary, conducting a give-and-take session. This is done by placing the author in the position of the one making a claim with proofs, and placing themselves as the reader as one asking a question. This method, however, can be undertaken like a student that has poor manners with their predecessors, such as one who says, "They are men and we are men also." It is better to place oneself in the position of one seeking an answer and simply narrating a question on behalf of someone else. For example, the student may say, "What if someone refutes this way? What if someone objects like this?" This is the method that befits one who has proper etiquette with the pious predecessors, as ought to be the case. In fact, proper etiquette is absolutely necessary because true virtuousness lies with those who came before us. Every writer from whom we benefit from amongst the scholars are in reality our teachers, and the right of the teacher over the student is well-known and will be discussed in detail in the fifth section if Allah 🙵 wills. This type of give-and-take discussion is for the student whose intent is to gain, increase, or strengthen the ability of retention (istiḥḍār). As for the one whose intention is to gain practical knowledge and to solidify it with proofs, this methodology of give-and-take is not necessary for him to obtain his objective. Whoever has a clear mind and a good understanding such that they can depend on their own intellect, then there is no harm for this individual to depend on their own faculties in acquiring what they intend from practical knowledge and solidification. After acquiring what was sought after, they should repeatedly study it until it reaches the level of easy recollection. However, the one who cannot depend on his own understanding and intellectual capability should not engage in such give-and-take discussions as it is not beneficial for them. Rather, it is disruptive to the

وَيَجِبُ عَلَيْهِ بَعْدَ أَخْذِ الْخُلَاصَةِ وَتَقْرِيرِهَا فِي الذِّهْنِ أَنْ يَتَأَمَّلَ فِيهِ مِنْ جِهَةِ الْوَارِدِ وَالصَّادِرِ بِأَنْ يُنَزِّلَ الْمُصَنِّفَ مَنْزِلَةَ الْمُدَّعِي وَالْمُسْتَدِلِّ وَنَفْسَهُ مَنْزِلَةَ السَّائِلِ، إِنْ لَمْ يَتَأَدَّبْ مَعَ السَّلَفِ وَيَقُولُ هُمْ رِجَالٌ وَنَحْنُ رِجَالٌ، أَوْ مَنْزِلَةَ الْمُسْتَفْسِرِ بِأَنْ يُحَاكِيَ وَظَائِفَ السَّائِلِ عَنِ الْغَيْرِ وَيَقُولَ: إِنْ مَنَعَ مَانِعٌ أَوْ نَقَضَ نَاقِضٌ أَوْ عَارَضَ مُعَارِضٌ بِأَنْ يَقُولَ كَذَا وَكَذَا مَا يَقُولُ فِي الْجَوَابِ؟ إِنْ تَأَدَّبَ مَعَ السَّلَفِ كَمَا هُوَ اللَّائِقُ بَلِ الْوَاجِبُ؛ لِأَنَّ الْفَضْلَ لِلْمُتَقَدِّمِ، وَأَنَّ كُلَّ مَنْ نَسْتَفِيدُ مِنْ مُؤَلَّفَاتِهِمْ مِنَ الْعُلَمَاءِ فَهُوَ أُسْتَاذٌ لَنَا، وَحَقُّ الْأُسْتَاذِ عَلَى الْمُتَعَلِّمِ مَعْلُومٌ كَمَا سَيَجِيءُ التَّفْصِيلُ فِي الْمَقْصِدِ الْخَامِسِ إِنْ شَاءَ اللهُ تَعَالَى.

وَهَذَا أَيِ الْقَائِلُ فِي الْحَاصِلِ مِنْ جِهَةِ الْوَارِدِ وَالصَّادِرِ إِنَّمَا يَجِبُ عَلَى مَنْ كَانَ غَرَضُهُ مِنَ الْمُطَالَعَةِ إِمَّا تَحْصِيلَ مَلَكَةِ الِاسْتِحْضَارِ أَوِ التَّنْمِيَةَ وَالتَّقْوِيَةَ. وَأَمَّا مَنْ كَانَ غَرَضُهُ تَحْصِيلَ الْعِلْمِ بِالْفِعْلِ وَتَحْقِيقَ ذَلِكَ الْعِلْمِ بِأَخْذِهِ عَنِ الدَّلِيلِ فَلَيْسَ بِوَاجِبٍ بِالنَّظَرِ إِلَى مَرْتَبَتِهِ وَغَرَضِهِ مِنَ الْمُطَالَعَةِ.

وَمَنْ كَانَ لَهُ صَفَاءُ ذِهْنٍ وَجَوْدَةُ فَهْمٍ وَقُوَّةُ قَرِيحَةٍ بِحَيْثُ يَعْتَمِدُ عَلَى ذِهْنِهِ فِي اقْتِدَارِهِ عَلَى الْجَمْعِ بَيْنَ الْإِتْقَانِ وَالْإِيرَادِ فَلَا بَأْسَ أَنْ أَوْجَبَ ذَلِكَ عَلَى نَفْسِهِ بَعْدَ أَنْ يُحَصِّلَ مَقْصُودَهُ الْأَصْلِيَّ مِنَ الْعِلْمِ بِالْفِعْلِ أَوْ تَحْقِيقِهِ، وَبَعْدَ أَنْ يَصِلَ الْمُحَصِّلُ إِلَى مَرْتَبَةِ الِاسْتِحْضَارِ بِالتَّكْرَارِ.

وَأَمَّا بِدُونِ الِاعْتِمَادِ عَلَى ذِهْنِهِ أَوْ لَيْسَ مَعَهُ شَيْءٌ مِنْ قَبِيلِ مَا ذُكِرَ أَوْ

order of studies and he or she will lose sight of their intended objective. At this point, one should strive for the acquisition of knowledge and strengthening that which they know, and they will delay this discussion and debate to another study time.

Every student or researcher ought to study the primary texts of those trustworthy commentators. One should depend on those in their extrapolation and study their methodologies, how they formed sentences, how they studied, and how they understood it secondarily. Thereafter the student should analyse how they open the discussion and investigation into the words and meanings. Likewise, when one intends to study commentaries from any science, they should follow a scholar who is accepted according to the peers of their time and who wrote a marginal on that commentary. One should not begin with how authors wrote their commentaries, then how authors wrote texts, then study each of those and judge between them. Rather, the student should first study one aspect completely and attain mastery in that. If one does not have the capability to study from all of these perspectives in every type of field, they should then suffice by choosing that which is most appropriate and most important according to their current state, to the science which they want to study, and to which is most essential to them at their level. One should ask Allah 🕮 for noble enablement and for help to increase them. They should always repeat this prayer in their heart, both openly and quietly: "Oh Allah 🕮, increase me in true, correct knowledge." Truly He is the One who gives noble enablement. He is the Enabler, the Helper, and He does not deprive those who ask Him.

مَعَهُ شَيْءٌ مِنْ قَبِيلِ مَا ذُكِرَ فَتَكُونُ أَبْحَاثُهُ مِنْ قَبِيلِ الاشْتِغَالِ بِمَا لَا يَعْنِيهِ، وَمِنْ بَابِ ظَفَرَةِ النِّظَامِ مُؤَدِّيًا إِلَى فَوْتِ الْغَرَضِ وَضَيَاعِ الْمَرَامِ؛ بَلِ الْوَاجِبُ عَلَيْهِ حِينَئِذٍ أَنْ يَسْعَى فِي التَّحْصِيلِ وَالْإِتْقَانِ وَيُؤَخِّرَ الْبَحْثَ وَالْإِيرَادَ إِلَى مُطَالَعَةٍ أُخْرَى.

وَيَنْبَغِي لِكُلِّ مُطَالِعٍ أَنْ يُقَلِّدَ فِي مُطَالَعَةِ الْمُتُونِ مِنْ كُلِّ عِلْمٍ شَارِحًا يَثِقُ بِهِ وَيَعْتَمِدُ عَلَيْهِ فِي التَّخْرِيجِ وَالِاسْتِخْرَاجِ، وَيَتَأَمَّلُ فِي صَنِيعِهِ وَفِي أَنَّهُ كَيْفَ يُصَحِّحُ الْأَلْفَاظَ وَالْعِبَارَاتِ أَوَّلًا، وَكَيْفَ يَأْخُذُ الْمَعَانِيَ مِنْهَا ثَانِيًا، وَكَيْفَ يَفْتَحُ بَابَ الْبَحْثِ وَالتَّفْتِيشِ مِنْ جِهَةِ اللَّفْظِ وَالْمَعْنَى ثَالِثًا.

وَكَذَا يُقَلِّدُ فِي مُطَالَعَةِ الشُّرُوحِ مِنْ كُلِّ عِلْمٍ مُحَشِّيًا مُسَلَّمًا عِنْدَهُ وَيُلَاحَظُ كَيْفَ يَتَكَلَّمُ تَارَةً لِلشَّرْحِ وَتَارَةً لِلْمَتْنِ وَتَارَةً عَلَى كُلٍّ مِنْهَا وَتَارَةً يُحَاكِمُ بَيْنَهُمَا. وَإِنْ لَمْ يَقْدِرْ مُطَالِعٌ عَلَى جَمِيعِ هَذِهِ الْمُلَاحَظَاتِ كُلِّهَا فِي كُلِّ مُطَالَعَةٍ يَخْتَارُ مَا هُوَ أَنْسَبُ وَأَهَمُّ بِالنَّظَرِ إِلَى الْمَقَامِ وَإِلَى الْعِلْمِ الَّذِي يُطَالِعُ فِيهِ وَبِالنِّسْبَةِ إِلَى نَفْسِهِ وَرُتْبَتِهِ. وَيَسْأَلُ اللهَ تَعَالَى التَّوْفِيقَ وَالْإِعَانَةَ عَلَى الزِّيَادَةِ وَيَقُولُ دَائِمًا بِقَلْبٍ حَاضِرٍ فِي سِرِّهِ وَعَلَانِيَتِهِ ﴿رَبِّ زِدْنِي عِلْمًا﴾ [طه، ١١٤/٢٠] بِالْحَقِّ وَالصَّوَابِ وَهُوَ الْمُوَفِّقُ الْمُعِينُ لَا يُخِيبُ السَّائِلِينَ.

Section Two

After taking into consideration the etiquettes that have been mentioned in the first section, the student should think about what they are seeking in general from the science they are studying. The student should then consider the area of study they are looking at and ask whether it is beneficial and whether it corresponds with their general intention and purpose. If they find that it is beneficial and helpful to their general purpose, they must ask themselves the question: would simple imitational knowledge without proofs suffice, or is a deep, investigative knowledge required? If the area of study is one of the auxiliary sciences not intended or sought after for themselves, such as etymology, grammar, meanings, expression, logic, or literature, then there is no harm in simply sufficing on imitational knowledge.

In such instances, imitational knowledge suffices because the discussions of these types of sciences are simply introductory concepts and set principles for sciences that are sought after in and of themselves. The salient characteristic of the fundamental introductory principles is that they should be accepted based on trust. Thereafter, when the student has attained the second level of study they can pursue further investigation into these foundational principles and the appropriate proofs for them. However, if the science being studied is sought after in and of itself, such as the sciences of theology or philosophy, then the student must seek a deep understanding based on proofs. One should not suffice with only claims and imitative knowledge because doing so will deprive the student of reaching their goal. However, if the area that one is studying does not contain proofs then they should seek out the proofs from another source after having first cemented the foundation of

الْمَقْصَدُ الثَّانِي

فِي بَيَانِ الْآدَابِ الْمُخْتَصَّةِ بِمَنْ كَانَ غَرَضُهُ مِنَ الْمُطَالَعَةِ تَحْصِيلَ الْعِلْمِ بِالْفِعْلِ

يَجِبُ عَلَيْهِ بَعْدَ أَنْ يَأْتِيَ بِالْآدَابِ الَّتِي مَضَى ذِكْرُهَا فِي الْمَقْصِدِ الْأَوَّلِ كُلًّا أَوْ بَعْضًا أَنْ يَتَذَكَّرَ أَوَّلًا مَا هُوَ الْمَطْلُوبُ عِنْدَهُ مِنَ الْعِلْمِ الْمَشْعُورِ بِهِ فِي الْجُمْلَةِ، ثُمَّ يُلَاحِظَ الْمَحَلَّ الْمُطَالَعَ فِيهِ هَلْ هُوَ مُفِيدٌ وَافٍ بِمَقْصُودِهِ أَوْ لَا، وَعَلَى تَقْدِيرِ كَوْنِهِ مُفِيدًا هَلْ يُفِيدُ الْعِلْمَ التَّقْلِيدِيَّ الْمُجَرَّدَ عَنِ الدَّلِيلِ أَوْ يُفِيدُ التَّحْقِيقِيَّ الْمُسْتَفَادَ مِنْهُ.

فَإِنْ كَانَ الْفَنُّ مِنَ الْفُنُونِ الْآلِيَّةِ الَّتِي لَيْسَتْ مَقْصُودَةً بِذَاتِهَا مِثْلَ الصَّرْفِ وَالنَّحْوِ وَالْمَعَانِي وَالْبَيَانِ وَالْمَنْطِقِ وَالْآدَابِ فَلَا بَأْسَ فِي الِاقْتِصَارِ عَلَى التَّقْلِيدِ التَّسْلِيمِيِّ فِي الْأَوَائِلِ؛ لِأَنَّ مَسَائِلَ تِلْكَ الْفُنُونِ بِمَنْزِلَةِ الْمَبَادِئِ التَّصْدِيقِيَّةِ وَالْأُصُولِ الْمَوْضُوعَةِ لِلْعُلُومِ الَّتِي هِيَ مَقْصُودَةٌ بِذَاتِهَا وَمِنْ شَأْنِ الْمَبَادِئِ أَنْ تُسَلَّمَ عَلَى سَبِيلِ حُسْنِ الظَّنِّ أَوِ الْجَدَلِ. ثُمَّ فِي الْمَرْتَبَةِ الثَّانِيَةِ وَثَوَانِي الْحَالِ عِنْدَ التَّرَقِّي يُطْلَبُ تَحْقِيقُهَا بِالدَّلَائِلِ الْمُنَاسِبَةِ لِفَنِّهَا.

وَأَمَّا إِنْ كَانَ الْفَنُّ مِنَ الْعُلُومِ الْمَقْصُودَةِ بِذَاتِهَا كَعِلْمِ الْكَلَامِ وَأَقْسَامِ الْحِكْمَةِ فَيَجِبُ عَلَيْهِ أَنْ يَطْلُبَ الْعِلْمَ التَّحْقِيقِيَّ الْمُسْتَنْبَطَ مِنَ الدَّلِيلِ، وَلَا يَقْنَعَ بِمُجَرَّدِ الدَّعْوَى وَالتَّقْلِيدِ؛ لِأَنَّ الِاعْتِيَادَ بِالتَّقْلِيدِ وَالتَّسْلِيمِ فِي تِلْكَ الْمَطَالِبِ يُورِثُ الْحِرْمَانَ عَنِ الْوُصُولِ إِلَى الْمَآرِبِ. وَإِنْ كَانَ الْمَحَلُّ الَّذِي يُطَالِعُ فِيهِ دَعْوًا مُجَرَّدًا عَنِ الدَّلِيلِ يَطْلُبُهُ مِنْ مَحَلٍّ آخَرَ بَعْدَ

that science through repetition. Thereafter, one should study the proofs closely alongside their conclusions. The student should carefully consider the benefit of the study, and practise the give-and-take discussions along with the rebuttals to potential questions as mentioned in the first section.

The student must restrict themselves to one section and one topic in everything they are studying, and review it time and time again. When the student has conceptualised the discussion from beginning to end, he or she should constantly consider the topic without visual aids, whether they are written words or diagrams. If the student is not capable of solely reviewing the meanings, then they have no alternative but to seek help by picturing the letters which indicate the previously learnt meaning. If one is incapable of that due to the closeness of the words, then one should verbally enunciate the words. The student should not restrict him or herself to only one language if they are bilingual, nor should they restrict themselves to the exact words of the source from which they have learnt. Rather, they should be able to articulate the meaning in their own words: the meanings of what you have mastered must become like an old friend that you recognise regardless of what they are wearing. Your knowledge of that meaning or reality should not be restricted to one language, one specific expression, or one specific arrangement. The one who keeps their knowledge or information in only one specific form has restricted their understanding of what they know and is considered a follower of the masses. This is something that not only causes stupidity and shallowness, but is in fact a sign of it.

One should not mix up one topic with another by advancing in studies before having solidified the first topic, making it firm in their mind, even if there is a type of compatibility between the two and they go together. This will cause confusion to the student, a deficiency in their learning, and stop the student from attaining perfection. However, if one is at a level where

إِتْقَانِ أَصْلِ الْمَطْلَبِ بِالتَّكْرَارِ فَيَتَأَمَّلُ مِنَ الدَّلِيلِ وَمُقَدِّمَاتِهِ وَفِي إِنْتَاجِهِ وَإِفَادَتِهِ الْمَطْلُوبَ حَقَّ التَّأَمُّلِ وَيُلَاحِظُ الْوَارِدَ وَالصَّادِرَ فِي دَفْعِهِ كَمَا مَرَّ فِي الْمَقْصِدِ الْأَوَّلِ.

وَيَجِبُ عَلَيْهِ أَنْ يَقْتَصِرَ عَلَى مَطْلَبٍ وَاحِدٍ فِي كُلِّ مُطَالَعَةٍ، وَيُكَرِّرَ فِيهِ الْمُلَاحَظَةَ وَقْتًا بَعْدَ وَقْتٍ وَحَالًا بَعْدَ حَالٍ بَعْدَ أَنْ يُصَوِّرَ مَضْمُونَ الْمَبْحَثِ مِنْ مَبْدَئِهِ إِلَى مَقْطَعِهِ فِي ذِهْنِهِ، وَيُكَرِّرَ التَّأَمُّلَ فِيهِ بِدُونِ اشْتِغَالِ الْحَوَاسِّ بِنُقُوشِ الْأَلْفَاظِ وَبِاسْتِمَاعِهَا. وَإِنْ كَانَ لَهُ عَجْزٌ عَنْ مُلَاحَظَةِ الْمَعَانِي الصِّرْفَةِ الْمُجَرَّدَةِ فَيَسْتَعِينُ بِتَحْلِيلِ النُّقُوشِ الدَّالَّةِ عَلَيْهَا، وَإِنْ عَجَزَ عَنْ ذَلِكَ أَيْضًا لِشِدَّةِ الْإِلْفِ بِالْأَلْفَاظِ فَيُجَاهِرُ نَفْسَهُ بِأَلْفَاظٍ وَلَا يَقْتَصِرُ عَلَى لُغَةٍ بِعَيْنِهَا وَلَا عَلَى لَفْظِ الْمُصَنِّفِ وَعِبَارَتِهِ بِعَيْنِهَا؛ بَلْ يُعَبِّرُ عَنِ الْمَقْصُودِ بِأَيِّ عِبَارَةٍ كَانَتْ مِنَ الْعِبَارَاتِ الدَّالَّةِ عَلَيْهِ بِالْوَضْعِ. وَيَنْبَغِي أَنْ يَكُونَ مُجَرَّدُ الْمَعْنَى عِنْدَهُ بِمَنْزِلَةِ صَدِيقٍ قَدِيمِ الْأُلْفَةِ بِحَيْثُ يَعْرِفُهُ فِي أَيِّ لِبَاسٍ رَآهُ. وَلَا يَكُونُ مَعْرِفَتُهُ لِلْمَعْنَى الْمَقْصُودِ مَقْصُورَةً عَلَى لُغَةٍ أَوْ عِبَارَةٍ مَخْصُوصَةٍ أَوْ تَرْتِيبٍ مَخْصُوصٍ حَتَّى إِذَا غَيَّرَ عَنْ تِلْكَ الصُّورَةِ كَانَ كَأَنَّهُ مَا عَرَفَهُ قَطُّ أَوْ عَرَفَهُ فِي الْجُمْلَةِ؛ لِأَنَّ مَنْ كَانَ يَعْرِفُ مَعْلُومَهُ بِصُورَةٍ مَخْصُوصَةٍ وَتَقْتَصِرُ مَعْرِفَتُهُ عَلَى أُسْلُوبٍ وَاحِدٍ يُقَالُ لَهُ: «تَابِعُ السَّوَادِ». وَهَذَا مِنْ مُوجِبَاتِ الْغَبَاوَةِ وَالْبَلَادَةِ؛ بَلْ مِنْ أَمَارَاتِهَا. وَلَا يَخْلِطُ مَطْلَبًا مَعَ مَطْلَبٍ آخَرَ فِي مُطَالَعَتِهِ قَبْلَ إِتْقَانِ الْأَوَّلِ وَتَقْرِيرِهِ فِي ذِهْنِهِ وَإِنْ كَانَ بَيْنَهُمَا تَنَاسُبٌ وَتَلَاؤُمٌ فِي الْجُمْلَةِ؛ فَإِنَّ ذَلِكَ يُشَوِّشُ الذِّهْنَ وَيُوجِبُ النَّقْضَ وَيَمْنَعُ عَنِ الْكَمَالِ.

they are mentally strong and possess lofty goals, it is possible to gradually progress from learning practical knowledge to deep investigative research, and then to knowledge retention or memorisation by repeating or by rote. Accordingly, the student will not need to undertake a second reading in order to grow and increase their knowledge. Rather, they will have reached that growth and increase in their first reading as a result of the strength of their mind and high aspirations. However, if one cannot trust their intellectual capabilities in all of these levels of acquisition, investigation, and retention, one must use their eagerness, aspirations, and abilities in accordance with their strength. If a student has the capability to acquire, verify, and solidify the knowledge, but does not have the ability to gain the requisite level of retention, they should delay the retention of the knowledge to another reading of this topic. However, if the student cannot do all of them, then they should exert themselves solely in knowledge acquisition, working to solidify what has been learnt and make it strong in their mind. Afterwards, they should research and investigate deeper by completing a second reading. In the third reading, they will work on their retention capability, giving each level its due. The student should refrain from over-burdening their mind with that which is above its capacity because this will cause them to desist in their studies and become bored before attaining perfection. We ask Allah ﷻ for enablement and help in every situation.

إِنْ كَانَ صَاحِبُ هَذِهِ الْمَرْتَبَةِ صَاحِبَ ذِهْنٍ قَوِيٍّ وَهِمَّةٍ عَالِيَةٍ أَمْكَنَ لَهُ أَنْ يَتَدَرَّجَ مِنْ تَحْصِيلِ الْعِلْمِ بِالْفِعْلِ إِلَى التَّحْقِيقِ ثُمَّ مِنْهُ إِلَى الِاسْتِحْضَارِ بِالتَّكْرَارِ فَلَا يَحْتَاجُ بَعْدَ ذَلِكَ إِلَى مُطَالَعَةٍ لِلتَّتْمِيمِ؛ بَلْ لِلتَّنْمِيَةِ وَالتَّقْوِيَةِ، فَإِنَّهُ كَانَ قَدْ وَصَلَ مِنَ الرُّتْبَةِ الْأُولَى إِلَى الرَّابِعَةِ بِقُوَّةِ الذِّهْنِ وَعُلُوِّ الْهِمَّةِ.

وَأَمَّا إِنْ كَانَ لَا يَعْتَمِدُ عَلَى ذِهْنِهِ فِي ذَلِكَ أَيْ فِي جَمِيعِ التَّحْصِيلِ وَالتَّحْقِيقِ وَالِاسْتِحْضَارِ فَيَصْرِفُ هِمَّتَهُ وَسَعْيَهُ بِحَسَبِ قُوَّتِهِ إِنْ كَانَ تَفِي بِجَمِيعِ التَّحْصِيلِ وَالتَّحْقِيقِ فَقَطْ بِدُونِ الِاسْتِحْضَارِ فَيَسْعَى فِيهِمَا وَيُؤَخِّرُ الِاسْتِحْضَارَ إِلَى مُطَالَعَةٍ أُخْرَى.

وَإِنْ لَمْ تَفِ بِجَمِيعِهِمَا أَيْضًا فَيَجِدُّ فِي التَّحْصِيلِ وَتَقْرِيرِ الْمُحَصَّلِ وَتَمْكِينِهِ فِي ذِهْنِهِ حَقَّ التَّمْكِينِ ثُمَّ يُحَقِّقُهُ فِي مُطَالَعَةٍ أُخْرَى ثُمَّ يَسْتَحْضِرُهُ فِي الثَّالِثَةِ مَعَ إِعْطَاءِ كُلِّ مَرْتَبَةٍ حَقَّهَا وَيَحْتَرِزُ عَنِ التَّكَلُّفِ وَتَكْلِيفِ الذِّهْنِ مَا لَا يُطِيقُهُ؛ فَإِنَّهُ يُورِثُ الْكَلَالَ وَالْمَلَالَ قَبْلَ الْبُلُوغِ إِلَى الْكَمَالِ، وَنَسْأَلُ اللهَ التَّوْفِيقَ وَالْإِعَانَةَ فِي كُلِّ حَالٍ.

Section Three

THE ETIQUETTES OF LEARNING FOR ONE SEEKING

VERIFIABLE KNOWLEDGE BASED ON PROOFS

Seeking verifiable knowledge based on proofs refers to the verification of knowledge, or authentication of its understanding, by learning the proofs for a particular subject. In order to achieve such a level of knowing, the student must contemplate the subject matter. One must ponder if this knowledge is an auxiliary science or if it is an intrinsically desired science. If it is auxiliary, the student must question whether it is based on proofs, or on simple imitation and acceptance for that which there are no proofs. For example, the questions of grammar and some of the rulings of etymology and logic are certainly based on proofs. Conversely, lexicology, as discussed in the first section, is contested as to its status as a science at all. The science of the Arabic language is contested in this manner due to a superficial consideration of the subject. However, in reality it is a science based on proofs from previous examples in the language. If we were now to consider it an auxiliary science not based on proofs, then the one studying it simply needs to gain proficiency and expertise by reading the trusted books in this field and from learning under the trusted experts. One does not need to busy oneself with searching for proofs. On the other hand, if it is an auxiliary science that has the capacity of verification based on proofs, then it is like other sciences such as word derivation and etymology, and can be verified by learning other examples, similarities, applications, and implementations of the correct principles. Such a categorisation is supported by Ibn Jinnī in his book, *al-Khaṣāʾiṣ*, where he narrates from his teacher Ibn ʿAlī al-Fārisī that, "Analogical arguments are used in the science of language, just as they are used in the science of derivation of words and etymology and grammar. From this, it follows that if we need a four-letter word with the root letters

الْمَقْصَدُ الثَّالِثُ

فِي بَيَانِ الْآدَابِ الْمُخْتَصَّةِ بِمَنْ كَانَ غَرَضُهُ مِنَ الْمُطَالَعَةِ هُوَ الْعِلْمُ التَّحْقِيقِيُّ الْمَأْخُوذُ مِنَ الدَّلِيلِ أَعْنِي تَحْقِيقَ عِلْمِهِ الْحَاصِلِ بِأَخْذِهِ مِنَ الدَّلِيلِ

يَجِبُ عَلَيْهِ أَوَّلًا أَنْ يَتَأَمَّلَ فِي مَعْلُومَاتِهِ وَعُلُومِهِ الَّتِي يُرِيدُ أَنْ يُوصِلَهَا إِلَى مَرْتَبَةِ التَّحْقِيقِ بِأَخْذِهَا مِنَ الْأَدِلَّةِ هَلْ هِيَ مِنَ الْعُلُومِ الْآلِيَّةِ أَوْ مِنَ الْعُلُومِ الْمَقْصُودَةِ لِذَوَاتِهَا؟ وَعَلَى تَقْدِيرِ كَوْنِهَا مِنَ الْأُوَلى هَلْ هِيَ مِمَّا يُقَامُ عَلَيْهِ الدَّلِيلُ مِثْلُ مَسَائِلِ النَّحْوِ وَبَعْضِ مَسَائِلِ التَّصْرِيفِ وَالْمَنْطِقِ أَمْ هِيَ مِمَّا يُضْبَطُ عَلَى حَالَةٍ تَقْلِيدًا وَتَسْلِيمًا وَفَضْلًا وَلَا يُقَامُ عَلَيْهِ الدَّلِيلُ مِثْلُ عِلْمِ اللُّغَةِ؛ فَإِنَّهُ قَدِ اخْتُلِفَ فِي كَوْنِهِ عِلْمًا فَضْلًا عَنْ كَوْنِهِ مُدَلَّلًا، هٰذَا فِي ظَاهِرِ النَّظَرِ وَإِلَّا فَفِي الْحَقِيقَةِ هُوَ عِلْمٌ يُسْتَدَلُّ فِيهِ بِطَرِيقِ التَّمْثِيلِ كَمَا سَبَقَ فِي الْمُقَدِّمَةِ فَلْيَتَذَكَّرْ.

فَعَلَى مُقْتَضَى الظَّاهِرِ الْمُطَالِعُ فِيهِ ضَبْطُهُ وَإِتْقَانُهُ بِأَخْذِهِ مِنَ الْكُتُبِ الْمَوْثُوقِ بِهَا أَوْ مِنَ الْمَشَايِخِ الْمَوْثُوقِ بِهِمْ وَأَنْ لَا يَشْتَغِلَ بِطَلَبِ الدَّلِيلِ وَالشَّاهِدِ. وَأَمَّا عَلَى مُوجِبِ التَّحْقِيقِ فَهُوَ فِي مَرْتَبَةِ عِلْمِ الِاشْتِقَاقِ وَالتَّصْرِيفِ فِي تَحْقِيقِهِ بِالشَّوَاهِدِ وَالنَّظَائِرِ وَتَوْجِيهِهِ بِالْوُجُوهِ الْمُنَاسِبَةِ. وَيُؤَيِّدُ ذٰلِكَ مَا ذَكَرَهُ ابْنُ جِنِّي فِي الْخَصَائِصِ نَاقِلًا عَنْ أُسْتَاذِهِ أَبِي عَلِيٍّ الْفَارِسِيِّ مِنْ أَنَّ اللُّغَةَ يَجْرِي فِيهَا الْقِيَاسُ كَمَا يَجْرِي فِي الِاشْتِقَاقِ وَالصَّرْفِ وَالنَّحْوِ. مِثْلُ ذٰلِكَ بِأَنَّا إِذَا احْتَجْنَا إِلَى كَلِمَةٍ رُبَاعِيَّةٍ مِنْ مَادَّةِ

of *ḍād*, *rāʾ*, *bāʾ*, then it is permissible to take it from another word paradigm by doubling the *lām kalimah*, or the third root letter based on the analogical argument, which is well-known even if this word is not known amongst the Arabs." This is also proven in his book *Maʿrifat Masʾalah* where he states, "To understand a question by the Arabic language through analogical arguments and to give preference to the conclusions found through such methods is better than memorising a book and limiting oneself to listening and imitation."

If a person is studying from the books of etymology and word derivation, or from everything else that is based on these fields, they must refer back to a detailed text describing the appropriate guidelines for this science. One must then solidify knowledge of these principles and guidelines according to what is necessitated by the science being studied. If one is studying grammar, then the student should seek out the proofs and verify their knowledge by reviewing the books which cover that field. In general, one must look closely at the proofs, whatever they are, in any field. This is done by looking at the proof and questioning whether such a proof has been passed down through narrations, or whether it is based on consensus, analogical arguments, breaking the analogical argument for a preference, or presumption of continuity. One should therefore look closely at each one of these types of proofs based on what is mentioned by Ibn Jinnī in *al-Khaṣāʾiṣ*, as he has been exhaustive in his explanation therein. It is also recommended to read what is summarised by Shaykh Jalāl al-Dīn al-Suyūṭī in *Iqtirāḥ*.

If one is studying other auxiliary sciences that necessitate proofs, then seek out these proofs based on what is strongest: take the strongest proof and duly contemplate over its premise, as was mentioned in the first section. If one's study is a science in which proofs are not sought after at all, such as the sciences of history, anthropology and literature, then one can

«ضَرَبَ» يَجُوزُ لَنَا أَنْ نَأْخُذَ مِنْهَا «ضَرْيَبَ» بِطَرِيقِ تَضْعِيفِ لَامِهِ عَلَى الْقِيَاسِ الْمَشْهُورِ فِي الْإِلْحَاقِ وَإِنْ لَمْ يُسْمَعْ ذَلِكَ مِنَ الْعَرَبِ قَطْعًا حَتَّى قَالَ فِي ذَلِكَ الْكِتَابِ: مَعْرِفَةُ مَسْأَلَةٍ مِنْ مَسَائِلِ هَذِهِ الْعُلُومِ الْعَرَبِيَّةِ بِالْقِيَاسِ وَالتَّوْجِيهِ خَيْرٌ مِنْ حِفْظِ كِتَابٍ بِمُجَرَّدِ السَّمَاعِ وَالتَّقْلِيدِ.

فَإِذَا كَانَتْ مُطَالَعَتُهُ فِي كُتُبِ التَّصْرِيفِ وَالْاشْتِقَاقِ وَمَا يَتَفَرَّعُ عَلَيْهَا فَحَقُّهُ أَنْ يَطْلُبَ الْوُجُوهَ الْمُنَاسِبَةَ مِنْ وُجُوهِ الْمُنَاسَبَاتِ مِنَ الْمُفَصَّلَاتِ الْمُتَكَفِّلَةِ بِهَا فَيَتَحَقَّقُ عِلْمُهُ بِهَا عَلَى حَسَبِ مَا يَتَحَمَّلُهُ الْفَنُّ مِنْ غَالِبِ الظَّنِّ.

وَإِنْ كَانَتْ فِي النَّحْوِ فَيَجِبُ عَلَيْهِ أَنْ يَطْلُبَ الدَّلِيلَ وَالتَّحْقِيقَ بِأَنْ يُرَاجِعَ الْكُتُبَ الَّتِي تَتَكَفَّلَ بِذَلِكَ وَيُمْعِنَ النَّظَرَ فِي الدَّلِيلِ مَهْمَا يَسَعُهُ الْفَنُّ، فَيُلَاحِظَ أَوَّلًا أَنَّ الدَّلِيلَ مِنْ قَبِيلِ السَّمَاعِ أَوِ الْإِجْمَاعِ أَوِ الْقِيَاسِ أَوِ الْاسْتِحْسَانِ أَوِ الْاسْتِصْحَابِ الْحَالِ، وَيَنْظُرَ فِي كُلِّ وَاحِدٍ مِنْهَا عَلَى مَا يَلِيقُ بِهِ مِنَ النَّظَرِ عَلَى مَا ذَكَرَهُ ابْنُ جِنِّي وَاسْتَوْفَاهُ فِي الْخَصَائِصِ وَعَلَى مَا لَخَّصَهُ الشَّيْخُ جَلَالُ الدِّينِ السُّيُوطِيُّ فِي الْاقْتِرَاحِ.

وَإِنْ كَانَتِ الْمُطَالَعَةُ فِي سَائِرِ الْفُنُونِ الْآلِيَّةِ الَّتِي يَجِبُ أَنْ يُقَامَ عَلَى مَطَالِبِهَا الْأَدِلَّةُ، يَطْلُبُ فِي كُلٍّ مِنْهَا عَلَى مَطْلُوبِهِ مِنَ الْأَدِلَّةِ أَقْوَاهَا وَيَتَأَمَّلُ فِي مُقَدِّمَاتِ الدَّلِيلِ حَقَّ التَّأَمُّلِ عَلَى مَا سَبَقَتِ الْإِشَارَةُ إِلَيْهِ فِي الْمَقْصِدِ الْأَوَّلِ.

simply verify these sciences and acquire expertise by memorising its knowledge. If one would like to evaluate these sciences, then extrapolate subtleties and new perspectives regarding the organisation and formatting of the work. This is achieved by extrapolating figurative, metaphorical, and implicit meanings and taking into consideration the special attributes and aspects of rhetoric that are mentioned by masters in the field of rhetoric. The fullest extent of mastery that a student can achieve in these sciences is accomplished by using examples and reference points to prove the perspectives that they are trying to show from the subtleties in the source. However, the science of juristic principles, for example, contains considerable scope for debate and discussion. Such discussions take place in the books of argumentation and debate, and also in the commentaries of the books of jurisprudence. It is therefore necessary for one to seek a proof for every question or problem within a question, and look closely at the proofs' veracity.

The sciences which are intrinsically desired, and for which a proof is sought after, are generally of three types: where the requisite proof is from the rational proofs only, where it is from the traditional and passed-down proofs only, or where it is from a combination of both of them.

1. An example of a science that is based solely on rational proofs is the science of philosophy.
2. An example of a science that is based solely on passed-on tradition is that of ʿaqāʾid, the science of Islamic creed according to the early scholars.
3. An example of a combined science is that of ʿilm al-kalām, which is Islamic theology or creed according to the later scholars.

The next category from the intrinsically desired sciences are those in which a proof is not prima facie sought after, however a proof is sought after in reality. An example of this is tafsīr (Qur'anic exegesis); there is no need for proofs in this

وَإِنْ كَانَتْ مُطَالَعَتُهُ فِي عُلُومٍ لَا يُطْلَبُ فِيهَا دَلِيلًا أَصْلًا مِثْلَ عِلْمِ التَّارِيخِ وَ أَيَّامِ الْعَرَبِ وَسَائِرِ الْمُحَاضَرَاتِ وَالْأَبْيَاتِ مِنَ النَّظْمِ وَالنَّثْرِ، فَتَحْقِيقُ أَمْثَالِ هَذِهِ الْعُلُومِ ضَبْطُهَا وَحِفْظُهَا عَلَى مَا سَمِعَ وَتَدْقِيقُهَا هُوَ اسْتِخْرَاجُ الْمَزَايَا وَالْأَبْكَارِ مِنَ النَّظْمِ وَالنَّثْرِ وَاسْتِخْرَاجُ الْمَعَانِي الْمَجَازِيَّةِ وَالْكِنَائِيَّةِ الْعَرَضِيَّةِ وَمُرَاعَاةُ الْخُصُوصِيَّاتِ وَالِاعْتِبَارَاتِ الْمُتَدَاوَلَةِ الْمُعْتَبَرَةِ بَيْنَ الْفُصَحَاءِ وَالْبُلَغَاءِ، وَغَايَةُ مَا يُحْتَاجُ إِلَيْهِ فِي أَمْثَالِ هَذِهِ الْعُلُومِ هُوَ الشَّوَاهِدُ وَالنَّظَائِرُ لِيُعْلَمَ مِنْهَا اعْتِبَارُ تِلْكَ الْخُصُوصِيَّةِ عِنْدَهُمْ.

وَإِنْ كَانَتْ فِي أُصُولِ الْفِقْهِ فَفِيهَا مَجَالُ الْبَحْثِ وَالنَّظَرِ وَاسِعٌ عَلَى طَرِيقِهِمُ الْمُبَيَّنِ فِي كُتُبِ الْجَدَلِ وَفِي أَوَاخِرِ كُتُبِ الْأُصُولِ. فَيَجِبُ أَنْ يُطْلَبَ دَلِيلًا فِي كُلِّ مَسْأَلَةٍ مِنْ مَسَائِلِهَا وَيُمْعِنَ النَّظَرَ فِي الدَّلِيلِ.

أَمَّا عَلَى تَقْدِيرِ كَوْنِ عُلُومِهِ مِنَ الْعُلُومِ الْمَقْصُودَةِ لِذَوَاتِهَا فِي ثَلَاثَةِ أَقْسَامٍ: [١] قِسْمٌ مِنْهَا: يُطْلَبُ فِيهِ الدَّلِيلُ عَلَى كُلِّ مَطْلَبٍ مِنْهُ ظَاهِرًا أَوْحَقِيقَةً سَوَاءٌ كَانَ الدَّلِيلُ مِنَ الْعَقْلِيَّاتِ الصِّرْفَةِ أَوْ مِنَ النَّقْلِيَّاتِ وَالسَّمْعِيَّاتِ الْمَحْضَةِ أَوْ مَمْزُوجًا مِنْهُمَا مِثْلُ الْعُلُومِ الْحِكْمِيَّةِ وَمَا يَتَفَرَّعُ عَلَيْهَا وَمِثْلُ عِلْمِ الْعَقَائِدِ عِنْدَ الْمُتَقَدِّمِينَ وَمِثْلُ عِلْمِ الْكَلَامِ عِنْدَ الْمُتَأَخِّرِينَ وَمِثْلُ فُرُوعِ الْفِقْهِ الْمُدَلَّلَةِ بِالْأُصُولِ. فَيَجِبُ عَلَيْهِ أَنْ يُطْلَبَ فِي كُلِّ وَاحِدٍ مِنْ هَذِهِ الْعُلُومِ مَا يَقْتَضِيهِ مِنَ الْأَدِلَّةِ وَأَنْ يَتَأَمَّلَ فِي الدَّلِيلِ بِحَسَبِ تَحَمُّلِهِ.

[٢] وَقِسْمٌ مِنْهَا: لَا يُطْلَبُ فِيهِ الدَّلِيلُ ظَاهِرًا وَيُطْلَبُ حَقِيقَةً مِثْلَ عِلْمِ التَّفْسِيرِ؛ فَإِنَّهُ لَا مِسَاسَ لِلدَّلِيلِ فِيهِ بِحَسَبِ الظَّاهِرِ إِلَّا أَنَّ كُلَّ مَعْنًى يُخْرِجُهُ الْمُفَسِّرُ مِنَ النَّظْمِ الْكَرِيمِ يُطْلَبُ عَلَيْهِ دَلِيلٌ سَمْعِيٌّ إِمَّا مِنَ السُّنَّةِ وَالْحَدِيثِ، وَإِمَّا مِنْ أُصُولِ الْعَرَبِيَّةِ حَتَّى يُقْبَلَ مِنْهُ ذَلِكَ التَّخْرِيجُ وَيُسَلَّمَ

science according to what is apparent, but in reality an exegete who derives a meaning from the Qur'an will be asked to provide a proof in order to substantiate his statement. Such a proof will arise from that which is passed down by oral tradition or from the principles of the Arabic language. Only then will the derived meanings be accepted from the exegete and the *tafsīr* considered acceptable. This is why *tafsīr* is considered a science in which a proof is sought after in reality. Similarly, it is apparent that there is no need for proofs in the science of Hadith (Prophetic narrations). However, when a Hadith narrator attributes a saying to the Prophet ﷺ, he or she will be asked to provide a proof regarding its authenticity. The chain of transmissions must be shown to be authentic, single-source, well-known, strange, or any of the other categories of the chains of narration. If the Hadith narrator connects the words in the text to the one who said them with an acceptable chain according to the scholars of this field, then it will be accepted. If not, it will be rejected. This shows that the science of Hadith is really a science in which proofs are sought after and considered with respect to acceptance, rejection, criticism, and praise of the narrators of the Hadith. All of this is well-known according to the scholars of Hadith. As for the science of the principles of Hadith, it is an auxiliary science, falling into the broader category of the principles of jurisprudence and in truth a sub-section of that science.

The third category is that group of sciences in which no proof is outwardly sought after. These may be from among the auxiliary sciences or from the intrinsically desired sciences. However, I consider this category to be more closely tied with the auxiliary sciences, such as history and all the sciences of literature. These sciences are studied by people of high aspiration: those who study everything from the sciences in order to perfect themselves, or because it is something beneficial to learn, or because it is useful for the perfection of beneficial sci-

تَفْسِيرُهُ مِنْ أَنْ يَكُونَ مِنْ قَبِيلِ التَّفْسِيرِ بِالرَّأْيِ فَيَكُونَ مِمَّا يُطْلَبُ فِيهِ الدَّلِيلُ حَقِيقَةً. وَكَذَا عِلْمُ الْحَدِيثِ فَإِنَّهُ لَيْسَ بِحَسَبِ الظَّاهِرِ لِلدَّلِيلِ مَدْخَلٌ فِيهِ، لَكِنَّ الْمُحَدِّثَ إِذَا نَسَبَ الْحَدِيثَ لِلنَّبِيِّ ﷺ يُطْلَبُ مِنْهُ دَلِيلٌ عَلَى ذَلِكَ الْإِسْنَادِ الصَّحِيحِ مُتَوَاتِرَاكَاتً أَوْ آحَادًا مَشْهُورَاكَاتً أَوْ غَيْرَ مَشْهُورٍ أَوْ غَيْرَ ذَلِكَ مِنَ الْإِسْنَادِ. فَإِنْ أَسْنَدَ وَأَوْصَلَ الْمَتْنَ إِلَى قَائِلِهِ إِسْنَادًا مَقْبُولًا مُعْتَبَرًا عِنْدَ أَصْحَابِهِ قُبِلَ مِنْهُ وَإِلَّا رُدَّ عَلَيْهِ وَلَمْ يُقْبَلْ مِنْهُ. فَكَانَتْ عِلْمُ الْحَدِيثِ عِلْمًا يُطْلَبُ فِيهِ الدَّلِيلُ وَيُتَكَلَّمُ فِي دَلِيلِهِ بِالرَّدِّ وَالْقَبُولِ، وَالتَّعْدِيلِ وَالتَّرْجِيحِ حَقِيقَةً عَلَى مَا هُوَ الْمَشْهُورُ عِنْدَ مَشَايِخِ الْحَدِيثِ. وَأَمَّا عِلْمُ أُصُولِ الْحَدِيثِ فَهُوَ مِنَ الْعُلُومِ الْآلِيَّةِ وَكَأَنَّهُ مُلْحَقٌ بِأُصُولِ الْفِقْهِ وَبَابٌ مِنْ أَبْوَابِهِ.

[٣] وَقِسْمٌ مِنْهَا لَا يُطْلَبُ فِيهِ الدَّلِيلُ لَا ظَاهِرًا وَلَا حَقِيقَةً. وَهَذَا الْقِسْمُ يُمْكِنُ اعْتِبَارُهُ مِنَ الْعُلُومِ الْآلِيَّةِ وَمِنَ الْعُلُومِ الْمَقْصُودَةِ لِذَوَاتِهَا أَيْضًا. وَنَحْنُ اعْتَبَرْنَاهُ مِنَ الْأُولَى مِثْلِ التَّارِيخِ وَسَائِرِ عُلُومِ الْمُحَاضَرَاتِ؛ فَإِنَّهَا إِنَّمَا يُطَالِعُ فِيهَا مَنْ هُوَ مِنْ أَصْحَابِ الْجِدِّ وَهُمُ الَّذِينَ يَطْلُبُونَ كُلَّ مَا يَطْلُبُونَ مِنَ الْعُلُومِ لِتَكْمِيلِ النَّفْسِ لِكَوْنِهَا نَافِعَةً فِي تَكْمِيلِ بَعْضٍ. الْعُلُومُ النَّافِعَةُ مِثْلِ التَّفْسِيرِ وَالْحَدِيثِ، لَا لِكَوْنِهَا مِمَّا يُتَلَذَّذُ بِهِ أَوْ لِكَوْنِهَا مَرْغُوبًا فِيهَا عِنْدَ أَهْلِ الْهَوَى مِنْ عَوَامِّ النَّاسِ؛ فَحِينَئِذٍ يَكُونُ مِنَ الْعُلُومِ الْآلِيَّةِ الْغَيْرِ الْمَقْصُودَةِ بِذَوَاتِهَا، وَقَدْ مَرَّتِ الْإِشَارَةُ إِلَى مَا يَنْبَغِي لِلْمُطَالِعِ فِيهَا.

ences such as *tafsīr* or Hadith; those who do not study solely because it is enjoyable or attractive. Accordingly, these sciences are considered auxiliary sciences, not an intrinsically desired science. Mention has already been made as to how one should study these sciences.

As for particular disciplines whose knowledge is considered praiseworthy by the scholars, each one of these will be studied according to the fundamentals of the general sciences from which they are based, having due regard to their rulings, their need for proofs or lack thereof, and to their respective methods of study. We beseech Allah ﷻ for His enabling grace in regard to the basis of knowledge and its branches.

وَأَمَّا الْفُنُونُ الْجُزْئِيَّةُ الَّتِي يُعَدُّ الْعِلْمُ بِهَا مِنَ الْمَعَارِفِ فِي عُرْفِ الْعُلَمَاءِ فَكُلُّ وَاحِدٍ مِنْهَا مُتَفَرِّعٌ عَلَى أَصْلٍ مِنَ الْعُلُومِ الْكُلِّيَّةِ، وَرَاجِعٌ إِلَيْهِ فِي غَالِبِ أَحْكَامِهِ لِيَكُوتَ فِي الِاحْتِيَاجِ إِلَى الدَّلِيلِ وَعَدَمِ احْتِيَاجِهِ إِلَيْهِ وَفِي آدَابِ مُطَالَعَتِهِ تَابِعًا لِأَصْلِهِ، وَمِنَ اللّٰهِ التَّوْفِيقُ فِي أَصْلِهِ وَفَرْعِهِ.

Section Four

THE ETIQUETTES OF LEARNING FOR ONE WHOSE INTENTION IS TO GAIN THE ABILITY OF RETENTION BY REPETITION

First, it is necessary for one to take notice of the similarities between that which one already knows and that which one is intending to study, particularly from the perspective of claims and proofs. If the student finds that there is complete conformity between the two in every perspective, then this is encouraging. However, one may find some disagreement in the claim, in the proof, or in both of them together. Similarly there may be a disagreement in the words, in the meaning, or in both the words and meaning together. In each situation, the disagreements will be either complete or partial. These are the conceivable possibilities of disagreements.

As for the possibility of disagreement in both claims with respect to words and meanings, it is inconceivable except in the case of a mistake. Complete and partial differences are both conceivable for disagreements in words only, whereas a complete difference in meanings only is inconceivable, though partial disagreement is certainly possible. As for the evidence that words and meanings may be in complete or partial disagreement, this is because a point may be proven through different proofs and methods. Similarly, complete or partial differences are conceivable in regard to the words alone or to the meanings alone. When both words and meanings are taken together, then complete and partial differences are conceivable only for the words; a partial difference is possible for the meanings alone, whereas a complete difference is inconceivable.

If one finds a conceivable difference, then they must contemplate over the perspectives and circumstances of the difference until they can choose between the two sides, giving preference to the stronger of the two. If one cannot eliminate the dif-

الْمَقْصَدُ الرَّابِعُ

فِي بَيَانِ الْآدَابِ الْمُخْتَصَّةِ بِمَنْ كَانَ غَرَضُهُ مِنَ الْمُطَالَعَةِ تَحْصِيلَ مَلَكَةِ الِاسْتِحْضَارِ بِالتَّكْرَارِ

يَجِبُ عَلَيْهِ أَوَّلًا أَنْ يُلَاحِظَ الْمُطَابَقَةَ بَيْنَ مَا عِنْدَهُ وَبَيْنَ مَا فِي الْمَحَلِّ الَّذِي يُطَالِعُ فِيهِ فِي الدَّعْوَى وَالدَّلِيلِ. فَإِنْ وَجَدَ الْمُطَابَقَةَ فِيهِمَا مِنْ جَمِيعِ الْوُجُوهِ فَنِعْمَ الْمَطْلُوبُ. فَإِنْ وَجَدَ الْمُخَالَفَةَ فَهُوَ إِمَّا فِي الدَّعْوَى أَوْ فِي الدَّلِيلِ أَوْ فِيهِمَا جَمِيعًا. وَأَيْضًا إِمَّا مِنْ جِهَةِ اللَّفْظِ فَقَطْ وَإِمَّا مِنْ جِهَةِ الْمَعْنَى أَوْ مِنْهُمَا جَمِيعًا. وَأَيْضًا كُلُّ وَاحِدٍ مِنْهُمَا إِمَّا كُلًّا أَوْ بَعْضًا، هَذِهِ هِيَ الِاحْتِمَالَاتُ الْعَقْلِيَّةُ.

أَمَّا احْتِمَالُ الْمُخَالَفَةِ فِي الدَّعْوَى مِنْ جِهَةِ اللَّفْظِ وَالْمَعْنَى كُلًّا فَسَاقِطٌ إِلَّا عِنْدَ الْغَلَطِ. وَأَمَّا مِنْ جِهَةِ اللَّفْظِ فَقَطْ كُلًّا أَوْ بَعْضًا فَجَائِزٌ. وَأَمَّا مِنْ جِهَةِ الْمَعْنَى فَقَطْ فَسَاقِطٌ أَوْ بَعْضًا فَجَائِزٌ. وَأَمَّا فِي الدَّلِيلِ مِنْ جِهَتَيْهِمَا جَمِيعًا كُلًّا أَوْ بَعْضًا فَجَائِزٌ؛ إِذْ يَجُوزُ أَنْ يَثْبُتَ مَطْلَبٌ وَاحِدٌ بِأَدِلَّةٍ. وَكَذَا مِنْ جِهَةِ اللَّفْظِ فَقَطْ أَوْ مِنْ جِهَةِ الْمَعْنَى فَقَطْ كُلًّا أَوْ بَعْضًا جَائِزٌ. وَأَمَّا فِيهِمَا جَمِيعًا مِنْ جِهَةِ اللَّفْظِ فَقَطْ كُلًّا أَوْ بَعْضًا فَجَائِزٌ. وَمِنْ جِهَةِ الْمَعْنَى فَقَطْ بَعْضًا أَيْضًا جَائِزٌ وَكُلًّا سَاقِطٌ.

فَإِذَا وَجَدَ الْمُخَالَفَةَ الْجَائِزَةَ فِي الْجُمْلَةِ يَتَأَمَّلُ فِي وَجْهِهَا وَجِهَتِهَا حَتَّى يَظْفَرَ بِهِمَا وَيَخْتَارَ الْأَوْجُهَ الْأَقْوَى مِنْهُمَا إِنْ لَمْ يَرْتَفِعِ الْخِلَافُ بِالتَّوْجِيهِ. وَأَيْضًا إِنْ كَانَتْ يَقْتَدِرُ عَلَى اسْتِحْضَارِ الدَّلِيلَيْنِ جَمِيعًا يَسْعَى فِي اسْتِحْضَارِهِمَا، وَإِلَّا فَيَخْتَارُ الْأَقْوَى مِنْهُمَا فَيَسْتَحْضِرُهُ.

ferences through some type of preference, and possesses the ability to retain both proofs, then they should strive to memorise both of them. Otherwise, they should choose the stronger of the two proofs and memorise it. While memorising, it is also necessary for one to try and find a new benefit in the words or meaning of the text with each repetition. One should attempt to uncover a new meaning from the untamed sought-after meanings, so as to achieve two benefits through this method of study: knowledge retention and an increase in knowledge. This will cause the student to become from amongst the well-versed scholars.

Undoubtedly, meanings contain deeper realities, some of which are clear and others hidden. The learning capacity of an individual varies according to their ability to perceive and understand those meanings. Some students understand meanings quickly, others are slower in understanding, and others still will never understand certain meanings because of their subtlety, or because of a limitation of intellect, or due to a combination of both. Through this combined type of study, a student's intellectual capacity becomes clearer, as does their level of scholarship.

By memorisation, I am not referring to the simple repetition of the spoken or written words, nor of their associated meanings. This is a skill which everyone who knows the definition of a given set of words is capable of. Mere repetition of the spoken or written words and their meanings does not increase one's intellectual capacity. There are two methods of repetition necessary for information to reach the level of acquired knowledge. The first method is practical reading with application, whereas the second method is reading and reviewing. This is because some knowledge that needs to be retained is auxiliary, and not intrinsically desired. Auxiliary sciences will be retained by repetition and by looking over the works and repeatedly applying them. For example, if a student wants to retain the knowledge

وَيَنْبَغِي لَهُ أَنْ يَجِدَّ وَيَسْعَى لِأَنْ يَجِدَ فِي كُلِّ تَكْرَارِ الِاسْتِحْضَارِ فَائِدَةً جَدِيدَةً مِنَ الْفَوَائِدِ الْأَطْرَافِيَّةِ اللَّازِمَةِ، إِمَّا مِنْ جِهَةِ اللَّفْظِ أَوْ مِنْ جِهَةِ الْمَعْنَى، وَأَنْ يَصِيدَ فِي كُلِّ مَرَّةٍ مِنْ مُلَاحَظَاتِهِ مَعْنًى مِنَ الْمَعَانِي الْوَحْشِيَّةِ الْمُتَصَيَّدَةِ لِيَحْصُلَ لَهُ فَائِدَتَانِ: فَائِدَةُ الِاسْتِحْضَارِ وَفَائِدَةُ الِاسْتِزَادَةِ؛ فَيَكُونَ مِنَ الْمُحَقِّقِينَ الْمُدَقِّقِينَ؛ إِذْ لَا شَكَّ أَنَّ الْمَعَانِي لَا تَخْلُو عَنْ لَوَازِمَ بَعْضُهَا بَيِّنٌ وَبَعْضُهَا غَيْرُ بَيِّنٍ يَتَفَاوَتُ الْأَذْهَانُ فِي الْوُصُولِ إِلَيْهَا بِسُرْعَةٍ أَوْ بُطْءٍ وَبِعَدَمِ الْوُصُولِ لِحَقِّ اللَّازِمِ وَضَعْفِ الذِّهْنِ. وَبِهَا يَظْهَرُ الذَّكَاءُ وَمَرَاتِبُهُ لَا بِمَنْطُوقِ الْعِبَارَةِ وَالْمَعَانِي الْمُطَابِقِيَّةِ؛ لِأَنَّ كُلَّ مَنْ يَعْرِفُ وَضْعَ الْأَلْفَاظِ لِمَعَانِيهَا يَعْرِفُ الْمَنْطُوقَ لَا مَحَالَةَ عَلَى السَّوَاءِ فَلَا يَظْهَرُ مِنْهُ رُتْبَةُ الذَّكَاءِ.

وَيَنْبَغِي لَهُ أَنْ يَعْرِفَ أَنَّ إِيصَالَ الْمَعْلُومِ وَالْعُلُومِ إِلَى رُتْبَةِ مَلَكَةِ الِاسْتِحْضَارِ إِنَّمَا يَتَحَصَّلُ بِالتَّكْرَارِ وَهُوَ يَتَحَصَّلُ بِطَرِيقَيْنِ: أَحَدُهُمَا: طَرِيقُ الْمُطَالَعَةِ مَعَ الِاسْتِعْمَالِ. وَالْآخَرُ: هِيَ الْمُطَالَعَةُ وَالْمُلَاحَظَةُ فَقَطْ؛ لِأَنَّ الْعُلُومَ الَّتِي يُرِيدُ اسْتِحْضَارَهَا:

[١] إِمَّا آلِيَّةٌ غَيْرُ مَقْصُودَةٍ بِذَوَاتِهَا فَيَكُونُ اسْتِحْضَارُهَا بِتَكْرَارِ الْمُطَالَعَةِ وَالْمُلَاحَظَةِ وَبِتَكْرَارِ اسْتِعْمَالِهَا فِي مَوَارِدِهَا وَمَحَالِّهَا، مَثَلًا إِذَا أَرَادَ اسْتِحْضَارَ

of language, etymology, and the derivation of Arabic words, then he or she will continuously review the books that contain this knowledge. In anything that the student reads, they should make note of the singular words and their sources and meanings. Thereafter, they should note the method of deriving one word from another, how its original form is cited, how the derived word is taken from the original, which words are derived through analogical reasoning, and so on.

Similarly, if a student desires to take his or her knowledge of Arabic grammar to the level of retention, they must study the books of grammar multiple times. When reviewing and repeating the rules and possible forms for any subject, they should not be lazy in mentioning anything in the text that is related to grammar. One can apply this method to the sciences of meanings, expression, and logic, as we have explained in the first section. As far as those intrinsically desirable sciences, they will only be retained through study and review. There is no possibility for application of the subject matter in these particular sciences, so the student must avoid progressing from one subject to another until they have sufficiently retained the first.

Likewise, one should avoid moving from one science to another until they have sufficiently retained the first. There are, however, differences of opinion regarding attaining expertise in a particular field. Does expertise mean that one must be an expert in every single question relating to that field, or does it refer to another type of mastery attained after completing and perfecting the science itself? Groups have discussed both opinions, but I adhere to the latter. One's knowledge or scholarly recognition within a set topic does not mean that they possess knowledge of all of the particulars of that area. Rather, mastery of a field is a separate type of skill that is attained after acquaintance with all aspects of that field.

اللُّغَةِ وَالِاشْتِقَاقِ وَالتَّصْرِيفِ يُطَالِعُ كُتُبَهَا مَرَّةً بَعْدَ أُخْرَى، وَيُكَرِّرُ فِي كُلِّ عِبَارَةٍ تَرِدُ عَلَيْهِ بِذِكْرِ مَوَارِدِ الْمُفْرَدَاتِ وَوَضْعِهَا لِمَعَانِيهَا وَيَذْكُرُ كَيْفِيَّةَ أَخْذِ بَعْضِهَا عَنْ بَعْضٍ وَيَذْكُرُ صُوَرَهَا الْأَصْلِيَّةَ وَالْفَرْعِيَّةَ وَالْمُعْتَبَرَ بِالْقِيَاسِ وَغَيْرِهَا مِمَّا يَتَعَلَّقُ بِالتَّصْرِيفِ. وَإِذَا أَرَادَ اسْتِحْضَارَ عِلْمِ النَّحْوِ يُطَالِعُ فِي كُتُبِهِ كِرَارًا وَيُكَرِّرُ تَذَكُّرَ أُصُولِهَا وَوُجُوهِهَا الْمُحْتَمَلَةِ فِي طَيِّ عِبَارَةٍ وَارِدَةٍ عَلَيْهِ وَلَا يُهْمِلُ تَذَكُّرَ شَيْءٍ مِمَّا يَتَعَلَّقُ بِالنَّحْوِ مِنْ تِلْكَ الْعِبَارَةِ. وَقِسْ عَلَى ذَلِكَ اسْتِحْضَارَ الْمَعَانِي وَالْبَيَانِ وَالْمَنْطِقِ كَمَا أَشَرْنَا إِلَى ذَلِكَ فِي الْمَقْصَدِ الْأَوَّلِ.

[٢] وَإِمَّا الْمَقْصُودَةُ بِذَوَاتِهَا فَيَكُونُ اسْتِحْضَارُهَا بِتَكْرَارِ الْمُطَالَعَةِ وَالْمُلَاحَظَةِ فَقَطْ وَلَا مَدْخَلَ فِيهَا لِلِاسْتِعْمَالِ وَتَكْرَارِهِ. فَيَجِبُ عَلَيْهِ إِذَا كَانَتْ مُطَالَعَتُهُ فِي الْعُلُومِ الْمَقْصُودَةِ بِذَوَاتِهَا وَيُرِيدُ اسْتِحْضَارَهَا أَنْ لَا يَنْتَقِلَ مِنْ مَبْحَثٍ إِلَى آخَرَ حَتَّى يَسْتَحْضِرَ الْأَوَّلَ اسْتِحْضَارًا مُحْكَمًا مُتْقَنًا. وَكَذَا مِنْ عِلْمٍ إِلَى آخَرَ مَا لَمْ يَسْتَحْضِرِ الْعِلْمَ الْأَوَّلَ حَقَّ الِاسْتِحْضَارِ وَيَحْصُلُ لَهُ مَلَكَةُ الِاسْتِحْضَارِ فِي ذَلِكَ الْفَنِّ.

وَقَدِ اخْتُلِفَ فِي أَنَّ مَلَكَةَ الْفَنِّ هَلْ هِيَ مَجْمُوعُ مَلَكَاتِ مَسَائِلِهِ أَوْ مَلَكَةٌ أُخْرَى تَحْصُلُ مِنْهَا عِنْدَ تَمَامِهَا؟ وَذَهَبَ إِلَى كُلِّ وَاحِدٍ مِنْهُمَا جَمَاعَةٌ وَالْحَقُّ هُوَ الثَّانِي. وَيَدُلُّ عَلَى ذَلِكَ أَنَّ مَعْرِفَةَ الْمَحْدُودِ لَيْسَ عِبَارَةً عَنْ مَجْمُوعِ مَعَارِفِ أَجْزَاءِ الْحَدِّ، هِيَ مَعْرِفَةٌ مُسْتَقِلَّةٌ تَحْصُلُ مِنْ مَجْمُوعِ تِلْكَ الْمَعَارِفِ عِنْدَ تَمَامِهَا عَلَى الْقَوْلِ الْأَصَحِّ.

وَمِمَّا يَدُلُّ عَلَى أَصَحِّيَّةِ الثَّانِي وَيُوَضِّحُهَا أَنَّ الْكَيْفِيَّةَ الْمُتَوَسِّطَةَ الْحَاصِلَةَ مِنْ تَفَاعُلِ كَيْفِيَّاتِ الْعَنَاصِرِ الْمُجْتَمِعَةِ الْمُتَمَاسَّةِ الْمُتَصَغِّرَةِ الْأَجْزَاءِ وَهِيَ

In my opinion, mastery of a particular science is not the ability to master every single topic within that science; it becomes incumbent upon a student seeking the faculty of retention to learn the science independently. After having completed the study of all the topics of a particular field, they must then consider whether they have attained another type of mastery: mastery of the entire field itself. If they have gained that mastery, then this is excellent and entirely desirable. If not, then the student must determine what is preventing them from acquiring it. Is it because of an insufficient mastery of the various topics, or is it due to inadequate organisation between the topics that have been studied? If the reason is recognised, it must be resolved by any means.

There is a clear difference between the one who has mastered the particular questions of a science and the one who has mastered the science itself. When the one who has mastered the questions of a science is asked regarding it, they typically do not have a general comprehensive knowledge of every single question. Conversely, the one who has mastered the particular questions along with the science itself will generally possess a comprehensive understanding of all of the questions and will be able to discuss in more detail when questioned further. For such a master, it is as if the entire science is one comprehensive question which is comprised of different sciences and knowledge, as has been explained. This is the most exemplary and highest form of knowledge that one can possess pertaining to the particulars; it is the connecting point between general and specific knowledge.

Thus, the discussion is not about which knowledge an expert should focus on, but rather, how the two types of knowledge should be brought together. Admittedly, if the one who only possesses knowledge of the particulars is asked about every topic and question in that field, then they will have knowledge of many of the questions that were asked. However, when such

الَّتِي يُقَالُ لَهَا «الْمِزَاجُ» عِبَارَةٌ عَنْ مَجْمُوعِ تِلْكَ الْكَيْفِيَّاتِ الْمُتَفَاعِلَةِ بِالِاتِّفَاقِ؛ بَلْ كَيْفِيَّةٌ مُسْتَقِلَّةٌ حَاصِلَةٌ مِنِ اجْتِمَاعِ تِلْكَ الْكَيْفِيَّاتِ. فَمَنْ سَلَّمَ الْمُغَايَرَةَ هُنَا اضْطُرَّ إِلَى تَسْلِيمِهَا ثَمَّةَ إِنْ كَانَ مُنْصِفًا وَتَسْلِيمُهَا هُنَا ضَرُورِيٌّ فَذَلِكَ ثَمَّةَ هَذَا وَإِنْ كَانَ خَارِجًا مِنَ الصَّدَدِ؛ لَكِنَّهُ لَمَّا كَانَ لِمَعْرِفَتِهِ مَدْخَلٌ فِي تَوْضِيحِ الْمَقْصُودِ ذَكَرْنَاهُ إِجْمَالًا.

وَلَمَّا ظَهَرَ أَنَّ مَلَكَةَ الْفَنِّ غَيْرُ مَلَكَاتِ مَسَائِلِهِ عَلَى الْقَوْلِ الْأَصَحِّ وَجَبَ عَلَى طَالِبِ مَلَكَةِ الِاسْتِحْضَارِ أَنْ يُلَاحِظَ نَفْسَهُ بَعْدَ تَحْصِيلِ مَلَكَاتِ مَسَائِلِ فَنٍّ هَلْ حَصَلَ لَهُ مَلَكَةُ الْفَنِّ أَيْضًا أَوْ لَمْ تَحْصُلْ؟ وَإِنْ كَانَ قَدْ حَصَلَتْ لَهُ فَنِعْمَ الْمَطْلُوبُ، وَإِلَّا فَيَتَصَوَّرُ مَا الْمَانِعُ مِنْ حُصُولِهَا هَلْ هُوَ لِقُصُورٍ فِي مَلَكَاتِ الْمَسَائِلِ أَوْ هُوَ سُوءُ التَّرْتِيبِ بَيْنَ الْمَبَاحِثِ؟ فَإِذَا عَرَفَ الْمَانِعَ أَزَالَهُ بِأَيِّ وَجْهٍ.

وَأَمَّا الْفَرْقُ بَيْنَ مَجْمُوعِ الْمَلَكَاتِ وَبَيْنَ مَلَكَةِ الْمَجْمُوعِ أَعْنِي مَلَكَاتِ مَسَائِلِ الْفَنِّ وَمَلَكَةِ الْفَنِّ فَهُوَ أَنَّ صَاحِبَ الْأُولَى بِدُونِ الثَّانِيَةِ إِذَا سُئِلَ عَنِ الْفَنِّ لَمْ يَحْصُلْ لَهُ عِلْمٌ إِجْمَالِيٌّ بَسِيطٌ شَامِلٌ لِجَمِيعِ مَسَائِلِ الْفَنِّ. وَصَاحِبَهَا مَعَ الثَّانِيَةِ أَيْ صَاحِبَ مَلَكَاتِ الْمَسَائِلِ مَعَ مَلَكَةِ الْفَنِّ إِذَا سُئِلَ عَنْهُ حَصَلَ لَهُ عِلْمٌ إِجْمَالِيٌّ بَسِيطٌ مُحِيطٌ بِجَمِيعِ مَسَائِلِ الْفَنِّ وَيَخْرُجُ إِلَى التَّفْصِيلِ حَيْثُ شَرَعَ فِي الْجَوَابِ شَيْئًا فَشَيْئًا؛ كَانَ الْفَنُّ عِنْدَهُ مَسْأَلَةً كُلِّيَّةً مُشْتَمِلَةً عَلَى عِدَّةِ عُلُومٍ وَإِدْرَاكَاتٍ عَلَى مَا بُيِّنَ فِي كُتُبِ الْحِكْمَةِ. وَأَوْرَدَ مِثَالًا وَنَظِيرَ الْعِلْمِ الْوَاجِبِ بِالْجُزْئِيَّاتِ؛ فَكَأَنَّ هَذَا الْعِلْمَ بَرْزَخٌ وَوَاسِطَةٌ بَيْنَ الْعِلْمِ الْكُلِّيِّ الْإِجْمَالِيِّ الْمَحْضِ وَبَيْنَ الْعِلْمِ الْجُزْئِيِّ التَّفْصِيلِيِّ الْمَبْحَثِ لَا مِنْ هَذَا وَلَا مِنْ ذَلِكَ. نَعَمْ، إِذَا سُئِلَ الْأَوَّلُ أَيْ صَاحِبُ مَجْمُوعِ الْمَلَكَاتِ فَقَطْ عَنْ كُلِّ مَسْأَلَةٍ عَنِ الْفَنِّ يَحْصُلُ فِيهِ

an expert is asked about the entire science generally, then they will not possess the ability to answer.

We have now made this matter clear, and it is crucial to remain vigilant in this regard. There are many benefits of knowledge which branch off of this point. One must always say "My Lord, increase me in beneficial knowledge."

ذَلِكَ الْعِلْمُ بِتِلْكَ الْمَسْأَلَةِ الْمَسْؤُولِ عَنْهَا، وَأَمَّا عِنْدَ السُّؤَالِ عَنِ الْعِلْمِ فَلَا. وَلْيَكُنْ ذَلِكَ فِي ذِكْرِكَ؛ بَلْ نُصْبَ عَيْنِكَ فَإِنَّهُ مِنَ الْمُهِمَّاتِ الَّتِي يَتَفَرَّعُ عَلَيْهَا فَوَائِدُ كَثِيرَةٌ. {وَقُلْ رَبِّ زِدْنِي عِلْمًا} [طه: ٢٠/١٤٤].

Section Five

THE ETIQUETTES OF LEARNING FOR ONE WHOSE INTENTION IS TO INCREASE THEIR KNOWLEDGE OR STRENGTHEN IT FROM VARIOUS SOURCES

Increasing one's knowledge is conceivable and possible according to the consensus of the scholars. Strengthening one's knowledge is also agreed upon, however there is disagreement as to the possibility of strengthening one's discernment.

According to Imam Abū Ḥanīfah, discernment is something which does not have the capability of being strengthened or weakened. He claims that an unknown is always unknown, and it can never be known. He attempted to prove this position by stating that if something is known from one perspective, and then it is learnt again from another, then the knowledge has in fact multiplied and has not been strengthened. Knowledge from the first perspective is one specific type of knowledge, and knowledge from the second is another specific type of knowledge different than the first. Thus, the knowledge has multiplied rather than strengthened. If this statement were true, then it would not be possible to know anything. This is an example of circular reasoning; if a certain thing is assumed to be known from one perspective, then what is actually known is the perspective and not the thing itself. Moreover, the connection between the thing that is unknown and the taken perspective is also unknown: the knowledge of the connection is dependent upon knowing the thing itself. This is clearly circular reasoning.

The great researcher Naṣīr al-Dīn al-Ṭūsī differed from Abū Ḥanīfah's opinion in his book *Awāʾil Sharḥ al-Ishārāt*, in which he said:

"Indeed, the great researcher and commentator erred in that he did not differentiate between that which is

الْمَقْصِدُ الْخَامِسُ

فِي بَيَانِ الْآدَابِ الْمُخْتَصَّةِ بِمَنْ كَانَ غَرَضُهُ مِنَ الْمُطَالَعَةِ تَنْمِيَةَ عِلْمِهِ بِالزِّيَادَةِ عَلَيْهِ أَوْ تَقْوِيَتَهُ بِتَحْصِيلِهِ مِنْ طُرُقٍ شَتَّى وَيَأْخُذُهُ مِنْ مَآخِذَ عَدِيدَةٍ.

أَمَّا الْأَوَّلُ أَيِ التَّنْمِيَةُ فَهُوَ مُتَّفَقٌ عَلَيْهِ بَيْنَ الْعُلَمَاءِ. وَأَمَّا الثَّانِي أَيِ التَّقْوِيَةُ فَفِي التَّصْدِيقِ مُتَّفَقٌ عَلَيْهِ كَالْأَوَّلِ، وَأَمَّا فِي التَّصَوُّرِ فَقَدِ اخْتُلِفَ فِيهِ: فَذَهَبَ الْإِمَامُ إِلَى أَنَّ التَّصَوُّرَ لَا يَقْبَلُ الْقُوَّةَ وَالضَّعْفَ وَيَبْنَى عَلَى ذَلِكَ إِشْكَالًا بِأَنَّ الْمَجْهُولَ مَجْهُولٌ دَائِمًا لَا يَقْبَلُ التَّعْرِيفَ وَاسْتَدَلَّ عَلَى مَذْهَبِهِ بِأَنَّ الشَّيْءَ إِذَا عُلِمَ بِوَجْهٍ مَا ثُمَّ عُلِمَ بِوَجْهٍ آخَرَ فَيَتَعَدَّدُ الْعِلْمُ وَلَا يَتَقَوَّى إِذِ الْعِلْمُ بِالْوَجْهِ الْأَوَّلِ هُوَ الْعِلْمُ بِهِ، وَالْعِلْمُ بِالْوَجْهِ الثَّانِي عِلْمٌ بِهِ هُوَ غَيْرُ الْأَوَّلِ، فَتَعَدَّدَ الْعِلْمُ وَلَمْ يَتَقَوَّ وَإِذَاكَانَتِ الْأَمْرُ كَذَلِكَ لَا يُمْكِنُ أَنْ يُعْرَفَ بِشَيْءٍ؛ لِأَنَّهُ إِذَا عُرِفَ بِوَجْهٍ فَالْمَعْلُومُ ذَلِكَ الْوَجْهُ لَا الشَّيْءُ الْمَجْهُولُ؛ إِذِ الِارْتِبَاطُ بَيْنَ الشَّيْءِ الْمَجْهُولِ وَبَيْنَ الْوَجْهِ غَيْرُ مَعْلُومٍ؛ لِأَنَّهُ يَتَوَقَّفُ عَلَى مَعْلُومِيَّةِ الشَّيْءِ فَيَلْزَمُ الدَّوْرُ.

وَرَدَّ عَلَيْهِ الْمُحَقِّقُ نَصِيرُ الدِّينِ الطُّوسِيُّ فِي أَوَائِلِ «شَرْحِ الْإِشَارَاتِ» قَالَ:

known and visible and whose essence is knowable, and that which is known and visible secondarily. If someone conceptualises something from any perspective, it is the thing and not the perspective that one is conceptualising. The perspective is conceptualised and noticeable only secondarily. Thereafter, the perspective is only conceptualised to serve as a reflection of the conceptualisation of the thing whose essence is noticeable. Our conceptualisation of that thing from a different perspective strengthens our conceptualisation of the actual thing itself. From this, it becomes evident that knowledge, or conceptualisation and discernment, can be increased by the different perspectives by which a thing is studied."

This is a summary of the words of Naṣīr al-Dīn al-Ṭūsī, which I consider to be the most acceptable position.

As for strengthening one's affirmation and perfection, it is agreed upon by all scholars to be conceivable. Undoubtedly, when a judgement is demonstrated by one proof and confirmed by another, the result is an increase and solidification of that knowledge. Therefore, one who is mastering a particular topic, or any individual mastering any type of practical knowledge, must exert oneself completely. Attaining and strengthening one's knowledge is achieved by correctly exploring the areas which are intrinsically connected to the field, and thereafter by exploring all of the extremities of these areas. This is realised by obtaining more knowledge from many different sources. Thereafter, one should consider the topic in regard to its postulates and affirmations. Are there any questions that remain unresolved? If so, is a resolution possible?

If one does not find anything at all objectionable, this can be due to some level of perfection within one's self or within the author. It is indeed a great outcome and one should be grateful

إِنَّمَا غَلِطَ الْفَاضِلُ الشَّارِحُ مِنْ إِنَّمَا يُفَرِّقُ بَيْنَ الْمَعْلُومِ الْمَلْحُوظِ بِالذَّاتِ وَبَيْنَ الْمَعْلُومِ الْمَلْحُوظِ بِالتَّبَعِ، فَإِذَا تَصَوَّرْنَا شَيْئًا بِوَجْهٍ مَا فَالْمُتَصَوَّرُ بِالْقَصْدِ وَالذَّاتِ هُوَ الشَّيْءُ لَا الْوَجْهُ، وَالْوَجْهُ مُتَصَوَّرٌ مَلْحُوظٌ بِالتَّبَعِ إِنَّمَا يَتَصَوَّرُ الْوَجْهُ لِيَكُونَ مِرْآةً لِتَصَوُّرِ الشَّيْءِ الْمَلْحُوظِ بِالذَّاتِ ثُمَّ تَصَوَّرْنَا ذَلِكَ الشَّيْءَ بِوَجْهٍ آخَرَ يَتَقَوَّى تَصَوُّرُ الشَّيْءِ الْمَلْحُوظِ بِالذَّاتِ بِسَبَبِ تَصَوُّرِهِ وَمُلَاحَظَتِهِ فِي مَرَّتَيْنِ إِحْدَاهُمَا بَعْدَ أُخْرَى. وَعَلَى هَذَا الْقِيَاسِ يَزْدَادُ قُوَّةً بِزِيَادَةِ مَرَايَا الْوُجُوهِ. هَذَا خُلَاصَةُ كَلَامِ الْمُحَقِّقِ وَهُوَ أَدَقُّ وَأَحَقُّ بِالْقَبُولِ. وَأَمَّا زِيَادَةُ التَّصْدِيقِ قُوَّةً وَكَمَالًا فَمُتَّفَقٌ عَلَيْهِ؛ إِذْ لَا شَكَّ أَنَّ حُكْمًا إِذَا ثَبَتَ بِدَلِيلٍ، ثُمَّ ثَبَتَ ذَلِكَ الْحُكْمُ بِعَيْنِهِ بِدَلِيلٍ آخَرَ زَادَ قُوَّةً وَكَمَالًا ثُمَّ وَثُمَّ...

إِذَا ثَبَتَ هَذَا فَنَقُولُ هَذَا يَجِبُ عَلَى صَاحِبِ الْمَلَكَةِ فِي فَنٍّ أَوْ فِي مَسْأَلَةٍ؛ بَلْ عَلَى صَاحِبِ الْعِلْمِ بِالْفِعْلِ مُطْلَقًا إِذَا طَالَعَ فِيهِ أَوْ فِيهَا أَنْ يَجِدَّ وَيَسْعَى أَوَّلًا فِي تَحْصِيلِ الزِّيَادَةِ بِالِانْتِقَالِ الصَّحِيحِ إِلَى اللَّوَازِمِ وَالْأَطْرَافِ، وَالْقُوَّةِ وَالْكَمَالِ بِتَحْصِيلِهِ مِنْ طُرُقٍ عَدِيدَةٍ وَأَخْذِهِ مِنْ مَآخِذَ كَثِيرَةٍ.

ثُمَّ يَتَأَمَّلُ فِي الْمَبْحَثِ فِي تَصَوُّرَاتِهِ وَتَصْدِيقَاتِهِ هَلْ يَرِدُ عَلَى شَيْءٍ مِنْهَا سُؤَالٌ بِوَجْهٍ مَا أَوْ لَا؟ وَعَلَى تَقْدِيرِ وُرُودِهِ هَلْ يُمْكِنُ دَفْعُهُ أَوْ لَا؟

for its achievement. However, this can also arise as a result of a deficiency in the student; either due to a superficial study of the various connected fields, or due to a lack of attention to the writing, terminology, and formulated sentences used. It may be due to a deficiency in one's study of the topic, and the student's inability to comprehend all of its parts, conditions, and limits. Alternatively, the student may have summarised the materials poorly the first time they were studied, with the initial inaccuracies remaining firm in the mind thereafter. The remedy for all this is simply the continual revision and review of the subject, at first generally and then in detail and precision, paying attention to both the words and the meanings, until one achieves that which is desired by the grace of time and circumstance. When one has obtained what they are seeking, either initially or after many repetitions, the next step is that one must put the author in the position of a claimant and put themselves in the position of an investigator, as was explained in the first section.

One must audibly speak to oneself with words as if seeking answers from a question, or one may narrate questions to the author as if someone else is asking the question. For example, "If a person objects by saying such-and-such a statement, what would you say in reply?" One may also act as if they are debating with someone that holds a conflicting opinion. In this case, one will give replies from the perspective of the author by using the evidence and statements given by the author himself. One will continue to increase in the investigation, as well as in the questioning and answering, in accordance with his or her mental strength and to the level that the entire topic has been understood. This process should continue until one has reached a point of necessary agreement. These debates and discussions are more beneficial when audible as that which is said out loud at the time of debate assists the mind. Additionally, many things apparent to one speaking audibly are not apparent

وَإِنْ لَمْ يَجِدْ شَيْئًا وَارِدًا أَصْلًا فَلَا يَخْلُو: إِمَّا أَنْ يَكُونَ عَدَمُ الْوِجْدَانِ هٰذَا مِنْ كَمَالِهِ وَكَمَالِ الْمُصَنِّفِ فَنِعْمَ الْمَطْلُوبُ أَوْ مِنْ قُصُورِ نَفْسِهِ. وَهٰذَا الْقُصُورُ إِمَّا مِنَ الْقُصُورِ فِي مُلَاحَظَةِ أَجْزَاءِ الْمَبْحَثِ وَإِعْطَائِهَا حَقَّهَا فِي التَّحْرِيرِ وَالتَّعْيِينِ فِي مُفْرَدَاتِهِ وَمُرَكَّبَاتِهِ إِمَّا مِنْ جِهَةِ الْمَعْقُولَاتِ الْأُولَى أَوْ مِنْ جِهَةِ الْمَعْقُولَاتِ الثَّانِيَةِ عَلَى مَا سَبَقَ فِي الْمَقْصَدِ الْأَوَّلِ؛ وَإِمَّا مِنَ الْقُصُورِ فِي اسْتِحْضَارِ الْمَبْحَثِ بِحَذَافِيرِهِ وَأَطْرَافِهِ وَقُيُودِهِ وَشَرَائِطِهِ؛ وَإِمَّا مِنَ الْقُصُورِ فِي أَخْذِ الْخُلَاصَةِ مِنْهُ وَتَقْرِيرِهَا فِي الذِّهْنِ وَتَمْكِينِهَا فِيهِ حَقَّ التَّقْرِيرِ وَالتَّمْكِينِ. فَالتَّدَارُكُ فِي جَمِيعِ ذٰلِكَ هُوَ تَكْرَارُ مُلَاحَظَةِ الْمَبْحَثِ إِجْمَالًا وَتَفْصِيلًا لَفْظًا وَمَعْنًى وَقْتًا بَعْدَ وَقْتٍ وَحَالًا بَعْدَ حَالٍ إِلَى أَنْ يَظْهَرَ الْمَقْصُودُ بِفَيْضِ الْوَقْتِ أَوِ الْحَالِ.

فَإِذَا ظَفِرَ بِوَارِدٍ إِمَّا أَوَّلًا أَوْ بَعْدَ تَكْرَارِ الْمُلَاحَظَةِ نَزَّلَ الْمُصَنِّفُ مَنْزِلَةَ الْمُسْتَدِلِّ وَنَفْسَهُ مَنْزِلَةَ الْمُسْتَفْسِرِ أَوِ السَّائِلِ كَمَا مَرَّ فِي الْمَقْصَدِ الْأَوَّلِ، وَيُجَاهِرُ نَفْسَهُ بِالْكَلَامِ كَأَنَّهُ يَسْتَفْسِرُ عَنِ الْأُسْتَاذِ مُسْنِدًا وَظَائِفَ السَّائِلِ إِلَى الْغَيْرِ وَحَاكِيًا عَنْهُ بِأَنْ يَقُولَ مَثَلًا: إِنْ مَنَعَ مَانِعٌ بِكَذَا مَا تَقُولُ فِي الْجَوَابِ؟ أَوْ كَأَنَّهُ يُنَاظِرُ خَصْمًا فِي مُقَابَلَتِهِ ثُمَّ يُجِيبُ مِنْ جَانِبِ الْمُصَنِّفِ بِالِاسْتِعَانَةِ مِنْ بَعْضِ الْقَرَائِنِ الْمَقَالِيَّةِ السَّابِقَةِ أَوِ اللَّاحِقَةِ أَوِ الْمَقَامِيَّةِ أَوِ الْحَالِيَّةِ، وَيَتَرَقَّى فِي الْبَحْثِ وَالتَّفْتِيشِ وَالسُّؤَالِ وَالْجَوَابِ بِحَسَبِ اسْتِعْدَادِهِ وَقُوَّةِ ذِهْنِهِ وَإِحَاطَتِهِ بِالْأَطْرَافِ حَتَّى يَنْتَهِيَ إِلَى مَقْطَعٍ ضَرُورِيٍّ أَوْ مُسَلَّمٍ. وَهٰذِهِ الْمُجَاهَرَةُ أَقْطَعُ وَ أَفْيَدُ مِنَ الْمُنَاجَاةِ؛

when inaudible. This is because of the comfortability that one's mind may fall into when studying quietly.

This is supported by what has been narrated to me: that al-Sayyid al-Sharīf 🕮 once travelled to Egypt to study *manṭiq* under Shaykh Mubārak Shāh. When attending the gathering of knowledge, he asked Shaykh Mubārak Shāh to give him an individual lesson so that he could learn Imam al-Rāzī's *Sharḥ al-Shamsiyyah*. Initially, Shaykh Mubārak Shāh refused his request and put al-Sayyid al-Sharīf with the other students. At nighttime, Shaykh Mubārak Shāh would habitually make his rounds and walk by the rooms of his students in order to see their level of devotion and effort. He would also provide help to some students if he noticed they were in need. When he reached the room of al-Sayyid al-Sharīf, he heard the sounds of a debate from within, one asking and one answering, but the voice was the same. He looked into the room and saw al-Sayyid al-Sharīf debating himself. He was acting as if he was debating Shaykh Mubārak Shāh, sometimes asking questions and sometimes answering them, sometimes giving answers on behalf of his teacher and sometimes asking questions as if they were posed by someone else, all in order to protect the proper manners one should have with their teacher. When morning came and al-Sayyid al-Sharīf went to class, Shaykh Mubārak showed him great honour and placed him in the front of the other students. He would also pay close attention to the questions that al-Sayyid al-Sharīf presented to him. It is said that the *Ḥāshiyah al-Ṣughrā* is actually written by al-Sayyid al-Sharīf, and that he wrote the text while he was studying under Shaykh Mubārak Shāh.

An important lesson for a student to take from this story is that whoever has the ability and aptitude to achieve the like of this must do so. The student should travel from one continent to the next, seeking out teachers and scholars, and not become impressed with their own ability. One should never desist from

لِأَنَّ الذِّهْنَ يَعْتَادُ بِالْمُجَاهَرَةِ عِنْدَ الْمُنَاظَرَةِ فَيَظْهَرُ لَهُ بِالْمُجَاهَرَةِ مَا لَا يَظْهَرُ بِالْمُنَاجَاةِ بِسَبَبِ الْإِلْفِ وَالِاعْتِيَادِ.

وَيُؤَيِّدُ ذَلِكَ مَا يُحْكَى أَنَّ السَّيِّدَ الشَّرِيفَ قُدِّسَ سِرُّهُ سَافَرَ إِلَى مِصْرَ لِيَقْرَأَ عَلَى مُبَارِكِ شَاهَ الْمَنْطِقَ وَلَمَّا حَضَرَ مَجْلِسَهُ طَلَبَ مِنْهُ دَرْسًا مُسْتَقِلًّا مِنْ شَرْحِ الشَّمْسِيَّةِ لِلرَّازِيِّ. أُسْتَاذُ مُبَارَكُ شَاهَ فَلَمْ يُجِبْهُ إِلَى مَسْئُولِهِ لِاسْتِحْقَارِهِ فِي بَادِئِ النَّظَرِ وَجَعَلَهُ شَرِيكًا لِبَعْضِ الطَّلَبَةِ وَمَضَى عَلَى ذَلِكَ أَيَّامٌ وَكَانَ مِنْ دَأْبِ مُبَارَكِ شَاهَ أَنَّهُ يَدُورُ فِي اللَّيَالِي عَلَى حُجُرَاتِ تَلَامِذَتِهِ مُتَنَكِّرًا لِيَنْظُرَ فِي جِدِّهِمْ وَسَعْيِهِمْ وَيَمُدُّهُمْ بِبَعْضِ حَوَائِجِهِمْ وَلَمَّا وَصَلَ إِلَى حُجْرَةِ السَّيِّدِ الشَّرِيفِ قُدِّسَ سِرُّهُ سَمِعَ مِنْ دَاخِلٍ آثَارَ الْمُنَاظَرَةِ يَسْأَلُ وَيُجِيبُ وَالصَّوْتُ وَاحِدٌ فَنَظَرَ مِنْ بَعْضِ الْفُرَجِ إِلَى دَاخِلٍ فَرَأَى أَنَّ السَّيِّدَ قَدْ جَلَسَ بِالْأَدَبِ يُنَاظِرُ الشَّيْخَ أَعْنِي مُبَارَكَ شَاهَ بِطَرِيقِ الِاسْتِفْسَارِ تَارَةً يَسْأَلُ مُحَاكِيًا وَتَارَةً يُجِيبُ مِنْ جَانِبِهِ مُحَافِظًا لِلْأَدَبِ فِي السُّؤَالِ وَالْجَوَابِ وَلَمَّا أَصْبَحَ السَّيِّدُ وَحَضَرَ الْمَجْلِسَ أَكْرَمَهُ مُبَارَكُ شَاهَ غَايَةَ الْإِكْرَامِ وَقَدَّمَهُ عَلَى سَائِرِ الطَّلَبَةِ وَكَانَ يُصْغِي إِلَيْهِ بَعْدَ ذَلِكَ فِي كُلِّ مَا يُلْقِي إِلَيْهِ وَيُعْرَضُ عَلَيْهِ. وَيُحْكَى أَنَّ الْحَاشِيَةَ الصُّغْرَى لَهُ قُدِّسَ سِرُّهُ هِيَ الَّتِي كَتَبَهَا وَقْتَ الْقِرَاءَةِ عَلَى الشَّيْخِ.

يَجِبُ عَلَى الطَّالِبِ الْعَارِفِ أَنْ يَتَنَبَّهَ مِنْ هَذِهِ الْحِكَايَةِ عَلَى أَنَّ مَنْ لَهُ مَلَكَةٌ وَاقْتِدَارٌ عَلَى مِثْلِ هَذَا التَّأْلِيفِ الْجَلِيلِ يَرْتَحِلُ مِنْ إِقْلِيمٍ إِلَى آخَرَ

seeking knowledge by taking it from the mouths of ennobled teachers. A true student's fear of their own inabilities and inefficiencies should force them to increase their knowledge, not only by studying the works of scholars but also travelling to them directly and seeking the benefit that is gained by sitting in their presence, meeting them, and keeping their company. That benefit can never be obtained by mere study alone, even if it is an in-depth, comprehensive study undertaken by a capable and diligent student. It is therefore necessary for every student seeking perfection to be aware of his or her own neglect and inability. The student should have high opinions of their predecessors and of their contemporaries. They should see in them excellence and superiority, never looking down upon them because of their speech or apparent understanding. We discuss this in detail in the final counsel, God willing.

If one claims that the person who has gained the faculty of retention does not need to study the text in order to gain more understanding, but rather that they should suffice with remembering or recollecting that meaning which has been firmly established in the mind from what he or she has retained, I would reply thus: while the person who has gained the faculty of retention does not need to study the words to recall the field they have mastered, they still ought to do so in order to make retention easier.

Human beings, so long as they remain in a state of growth and development, find it difficult to grasp meanings alone. Rather, they grasp meanings through the use of words, or through the use of that which is similar to language in the ability to indicate meanings, such as pictures. They then explore the meanings of particulars by the means of contemplating and evaluating the meanings of generalities. If one requires words or their like in order to grasp meanings in the first instance, they will also need words or their like in order to grasp meanings the second time. The second conceptualisation of meanings is called *tadhak-*

لِطَلَبِ الْأُسْتَاذِ وَالشَّيْخِ وَلَا تُعْجِبُهُ نَفْسُهُ بِتِلْكَ الْمَلَكَةِ الْجَلِيلَةِ وَلَا يَتَقَاعَدُ بِسَبَبِهَا عَنْ طَلَبِ الزِّيَادَةِ وَالْقُوَّةِ بِطَرِيقِ الْأَخْذِ مِنْ أَفْوَاهِ الْكَامِلِينَ وَلَا يَقْتَصِرُ عَلَى الزِّيَادَةِ وَالْقُوَّةِ الْحَاصِلَةِ لَهُ بِمُطَالَعَةِ آثَارِهِمْ وَمُلَاحَظَةِ مُؤَلَّفَاتِهِمْ ظَنًّا فِي حَقِّ نَفْسِهِ بِالنُّقْصَانِ وَالْقُصُورِ وَاعْتِقَادًا بِأَنَّ الْفَيْضَ الْحَاصِلَ بِمُشَافَهَةِ الْمَشَايِخِ الْكَامِلِينَ وَبِمُلَازَمَةِ مَجَالِسِ الْأَسَاتِيذِ الْمَاهِرِينَ لَا يَحْصُلُ بِمُجَرَّدِ الْمُطَالَعَةِ وَلَوْ كَانَ الْمُطَالِعُ مُسْتَحْضِرًا فِيهِمَا ذَكِيًّا وَقَّادًا نَقَّادًا. فَيَجِبُ عَلَى طَالِبِ الْكَمَالِ أَنْ يُسِيءَ ظَنَّهُ فِي حَقِّ نَفْسِهِ بِالنُّقْصَانِ وَالْقُصُورِ وَيُحْسِنَ ظَنَّهُ فِي حَقِّ غَيْرِهِ مِنَ السَّلَفِ وَالْخَلَفِ بِالْكَمَالِ وَالرُّجْحَانِ وَلَا يَسْتَحْقِرَ أَحَدًا فِي قَوْلِهِ وَفَهْمِهِ كَمَا سَيَجِيءُ فِي وَصَايَا الْخَاتِمَةِ إِنْ شَاءَ اللهُ الرَّحْمَنُ.

فَإِنْ قُلْتَ: صَاحِبُ مَلَكَةِ الِاسْتِحْضَارِ لَا يَحْتَاجُ إِلَى مُطَالَعَةِ الرُّسُومِ وَالنُّقُوشِ لِتَحْصِيلِ الْمَفْهُومِ؛ بَلْ يَكْفِيهِ تَذَكُّرُ الْمَعْنَى الْمَضْبُوطِ عِنْدَهُ وَاسْتِحْضَارُهُ. قُلْتُ: إِنَّ صَاحِبَ مَلَكَةِ الِاسْتِحْضَارِ وَإِنْ لَمْ يَحْتَجْ إِلَى مُطَالَعَةِ النُّقُوشِ فِي أَصْلِ الِاسْتِحْضَارِ؛ لَكِنَّهُ يَحْتَاجُ إِلَيْهِ فِي سُهُولَتِهِ؛ لِأَنَّ النَّفْسَ النَّاطِقَةَ مَا دَامَتْ فِي هَذِهِ النَّشْأَةِ لَا تُقْدِمُ عَلَى إِدْرَاكِ الْمَعَانِي مُجَرَّدَةً صِرْفَةً؛ بَلْ تُدْرِكُهَا بِوَاسِطَةِ الْأَلْفَاظِ وَمَا هُوَ بِمَنْزِلَتِهِمَا فِي الدَّلَالَةِ عَلَيْهَا مِنَ الصُّوَرِ الْمَحْسُوسَةِ وَتَنْزِعُ مِنَ الْمَعَانِي الْجُزْئِيَّةِ بِوَاسِطَةِ الْمُفَكِّرَةِ الْمَعَانِيَ الْكُلِّيَّةَ وَلَمَّا احْتَاجَتِ النَّفْسُ فِي إِدْرَاكِهَا الْمَعَانِيَ أَوَّلًا إِلَى أَلْفَاظٍ أَوْ مَا هُوَ بِمَنْزِلَتِهَا احْتَاجَتْ إِلَيْهَا فِي إِدْرَاكِهَا إِيَّاهَا ثَانِيًا

kur, or retention, because both have the exact same meaning. Each means that the student can conceive or conceptualise that which has been firmly understood for a second time, and can separate it exclusively from all other meanings and ideas that are also firmly established in their mind. The person can recall the conceptualisation by means of their memory. However, this recollection is a recollection of that which indicates the meaning; a recollection of the words or the picture. It is achieved either by the primary method of written words, or by using one's mind or imagination. The recollection of these words or pictures is thereafter used to provide the secondarily sought-after meanings.

There are two methodologies for recalling those words or pictures which indicate meaning. The first is the use of sensory perception, in particular sight or sound. The second is to use one's imagination. However, the use of sensory perception is easier than imagination. Imagination, or conceptualisation, is to review those same words or indicators while they are in one's mind. This is, of course, a very general explanation. The detailed meaning of conceptualisation is that one breaks down an idea into its isolated forms which are then stored in one's mind. Thereafter, one chooses from those forms which coincides with what they are seeking, takes all of the forms together, and reorganises them in such a way that creates a grander more comprehensive form. This reorganised form should be harmonious with that which they initially learnt. That single general form is then used as a method to recall the original meaning.

Certainly, this conceptualisation method is more difficult as it requires more effort than the use of sensory perception. The sensory method is free from any strain or exertion. Due to this ease, one becomes comfortable and enjoys evaluating the meanings that have been retained, and exploring the things that are necessitated because of those meanings. These details make it clear that studying and reading has great benefit for

أَيْضًا. وَالْإِدْرَاكُ الثَّانِي هُوَ التَّذَكُّرُ وَالِاسْتِحْضَارُ؛ لِأَنَّ كُلَّ وَاحِدٍ مِنْهُمَا عِبَارَةٌ عَنْ إِدْرَاكِ النَّفْسِ الْمَعْنَى الْمَضْبُوطَ عِنْدَهَا ثَانِيًا وَعَنْ تَعْيِينِهَا إِيَّاهُ مِنْ بَيْنِ سَائِرِ الْمَعَانِي الْمَضْبُوطَةِ عِنْدَهَا وَاسْتِحْضَارِهِ بِوَاسِطَةِ الذِّكْرِ وَالِاسْتِحْضَارُ احْتَاجَتْ إِلَى اسْتِحْضَارِ مَا يَدُلُّ عَلَيْهِ مِنَ الْأَلْفَاظِ أَوِ الصُّوَرِ أَوَّلًا إِمَّا بِطَرِيقِ الْإِحْسَاسِ وَإِمَّا بِطَرِيقِ التَّخَيُّلِ ثُمَّ يَسْتَحْضِرُ بِمُعَاوَنَتِهَا الْمَعْنَى الْمَطْلُوبَ.

وَطَرِيقُ اسْتِحْضَارِ تِلْكَ الدَّوَالِّ أَيِ الْأَلْفَاظِ أَوْ مَا هُوَ بِمَنْزِلَتِهَا مِنَ الصُّوَرِ مُنْحَصِرٌ فِي اثْنَيْنِ: أَحَدُهُمَا الْإِحْسَاسُ وَالْآخَرُ التَّخَيُّلُ، لَكِنَّ الْأَوَّلَ أَيِ الْإِحْسَاسَ أَسْهَلُ مِنَ الثَّانِي أَيِ التَّخَيُّلِ؛ لِأَنَّ الْإِحْسَاسَ عِبَارَةٌ عَنْ مُطَالَعَةِ النُّقُوشِ الْمُرَتَّبَةِ الدَّالَّةِ عَلَى تِلْكَ الْأَلْفَاظِ وَالصُّوَرِ، وَمُشَاهَدَتِهَا حَالَ كَوْنِهَا مَنْقُوشَةً فِي الْقَرَاطِيسِ أَوْ فِيمَا يَقُومُ مَقَامَهَا وَالتَّخَيُّلُ عِبَارَةٌ عَنْ مُلَاحَظَةِ تِلْكَ النُّقُوشِ حَالَ كَوْنِهَا فِي الْخَيَالِ. هَذَا مَعْنًى سَطْحِيٌّ إِجْمَالِيٌّ لِلتَّخَيُّلِ، وَأَمَّا تَفْصِيلُهُ فَهُوَ عِبَارَةٌ عَنْ تَرَاجُعِ الْمُفَكِّرَةِ إِلَى الصُّوَرِ الْجُزْئِيَّةِ الْمَخْزُونَةِ فِي الْخَيَالِ وَتَنْتَخِبُ مِنْهَا مَا يُنَاسِبُ الْمَعْنَى الْمَطْلُوبَ ثُمَّ تُرَتِّبُهَا تَرْتِيبًا يَحْصُلُ بِهِ مَجْمُوعُ تِلْكَ الصُّوَرِ الْمُرَتَّبَةِ صُورَةً وَحْدَانِيَّةً كَانَتْ هِيَ عَلَيْهَا أَوْ عَلَى مَا يُمَاثِلُهَا أَوْ يُقَارِبُهَا عِنْدَ أَخْذِ الْمَعَانِي مِنْهَا أَوَّلًا، ثُمَّ تَعْرِفُهَا تِلْكَ الصُّورَةَ الْوَحْدَانِيَّةَ: هِيَ النَّفْسُ النَّاطِقَةُ فَبِوَاسِطَتِهَا تَسْتَحْضِرُ النَّفْسُ الْمَعْنَى الْمَطْلُوبَ، أَعْنِي تَنْتَقِلُ مِنْهَا إِلَيْهِ.

لَا شَكَّ أَنَّ هَذَا الطَّرِيقَ أَعْنِي طَرِيقَ التَّخَيُّلِ لَا يَخْلُو عَنْ كُلْفَةِ تَعَمُّلٍ وَاحْتِمَالٍ بِخِلَافِ الطَّرِيقِ الْأَوَّلِ أَيِ الْإِحْسَاسِ؛ فَإِنَّهُ خَالٍ مِنَ التَّكَلُّفِ وَالتَّعَسُّفِ فَيَكُونُ أَسْهَلَ وَبِسَبَبِ السُّهُولَةِ تَنْبَسِطُ النَّفْسُ وَيَحْسُنُ تَصَرُّفُهَا فِي الْمَعَانِي الْمُسْتَحْضَرَةِ وَانْتِقَالُهَا مِنْهَا إِلَى اللَّوَازِمِ وَالْأَطْرَافِ.

both the one who has already retained information and the one who wishes to increase in knowledge.

Regarding the definition of *muṭālaʿah*, or study, we can summarise the opinions by stating that it includes all the forms of indication, whether written or conceptual; where written includes that which is written on paper as well as that which is written on the mind. In either case, we see that study is a necessary component for retaining information, and Allah ﷻ is the facilitator of ease.

وَظَهَرَ مِنْ هَذَا التَّفْصِيلِ أَنَّ الْمُطَالَعَةَ لَهَا نَفْعٌ عَظِيمٌ فِي حَقِّ الْمُسْتَحْضِرِ الْمُسْتَزِيدِ أَيْضًا لِسُهُولَةِ الِاسْتِحْضَارِ بِهَا، عَلَى أَنَّ لَنَا أَنْ نُعَمِّمَ الْمُلَاحَظَةَ الْمَأْخُوذَةَ فِي تَعْرِيفِ الْمُطَالَعَةِ وَنَجْعَلَهَا بِمَعْنَى مُلَاحَظَةِ الدَّوَالِّ مُطْلَقًا سَوَاءٌ كَانَتْ تِلْكَ الدَّوَالُّ الْمَلْحُوظَةُ مَرْسُومَةً أَوْ مُخَيَّلَةً أَوْ نُعَمِّمَ الرَّسْمَ إِلَى الرَّسْمِ فِي الْقَرَاطِيسِ وَإِلَى الرَّسْمِ فِي الْخَيَالِ، وَعَلَى كُلِّ وَاحِدٍ مِنَ التَّقْدِيرَيْنِ يَثْبُتُ الِاحْتِيَاجُ إِلَى الْمُطَالَعَةِ فِي أَصْلِ الِاسْتِحْضَارِ، وَمِنَ اللهِ التَّسْهِيلُ وَالتَّيْسِيرُ.

A Final Word

**REGARDING MATTERS WHICH BENEFIT AND FACILITATE
THE ATTAINMENT OF WHAT IS SOUGHT AFTER, FROM THE
PERSPECTIVE OF PERFECTION AND COMPLETION**

It is necessary for every student to protect themselves from common mistakes in seeking knowledge and their causes. There are many reasons for mistakes and errors, so many in fact that they are impossible to enumerate. However, the majority of mistakes originate due to an inability to differentiate between two similar things. This may be in regard to words and terms, or meanings and concepts. Scholars have detailed certain prevalent mistakes and divided them into two categories: external mistakes, which are not directly related to the actual speech or written words, and internal mistakes, which are directly related. The scholars have not described external mistakes in great detail as there is little benefit in knowing these and they have not been fashioned into a precise discipline. However, they have discussed internal mistakes, dividing them into those dealing with terms and those dealing with meanings. Internal mistakes relating to terms were further divided into six categories, while the internal mistakes relating to meaning were divided into seven. Thus, the complete number of internal structural mistakes that can occur are thirteen.

Regarding errors in terms, there are those that are related to individual terms, such as the definition of the term being equivocal or unequivocal, or to the literal and figurative usage of words. The form of the word can be a form of *iʿlāl* (weakness) or a coalescent form. For example, take the word *mukhtār* (chosen), where the active participle is the same as the passive participle. Likewise, with the word *mudd*, the passive verb is the same as the command form. Lastly, the incorrect inflection of a word or a misspelling can lead to misunderstanding the text. Other errors are in relation to sentences or phrases, such

الْخَاتِمَةُ

فِي أُمُورٍ تَنْفَعُ مَعْرِفَتُهَا فِي الْمَقْصُودِ مِنْ جِهَةِ التَّكْمِيلِ وَالتَّتْمِيمِ

يَنْبَغِي لِكُلِّ مُطَالِعٍ أَنْ يَحْتَرِزَ عَنْ مَوَاقِعِ الْغَلَطِ وَأَسْبَابِهِ وَمَنْشَأِهِ. وَلِلْغَلَطِ أَسْبَابٌ كَثِيرَةٌ تَكَادُ أَنْ لَا تَنْضَبِطَ، وَمَعَ كَثْرَتِهَا تَرْجِعُ إِلَى مَعْنًى وَاحِدٍ وَهُوَ عَدَمُ الْفَرْقِ بَيْنَ الشَّيْءِ وَشَبِيهِهِ فِي اللَّفْظِ أَوْ فِي الْمَعْنَى.

ثُمَّ إِنَّ الْمُحَقِّقِينَ حَصَرُوا الْمَشْهُورَ الْكَثِيرَ الْوُقُوعِ مِنْهَا فِي قِسْمَيْنِ: خَارِجِيٍّ لَيْسَ فِي نَفْسِ الْكَلَامِ، وَدَاخِلِيٍّ فِي نَفْسِ الْكَلَامِ. وَلَمْ يَتَعَرَّضُوا لِلْخَارِجِيِّ لِعَدَمِ النَّفْعِ فِي مَعْرِفَتِهِ وَلِعَدَمِ انْضِبَاطِهِ بِضَابِطَةٍ. ثُمَّ قَسَّمُوا الدَّاخِلِيَّ إِلَى لَفْظِيٍّ وَمَعْنَوِيٍّ ثُمَّ اللَّفْظِيَّ إِلَى سِتَّةِ أَقْسَامٍ، وَالْمَعْنَوِيَّ إِلَى سَبْعَةٍ، فَصَارَتِ الْأَسْبَابُ الدَّاخِلِيَّةُ لِلْغَلَطِ بِحَسَبِ الِاسْتِقْرَاءِ ثَلَاثَةَ عَشَرَ سَبَبًا.

وَمِنَ اللَّفْظِيِّ مَا يَرْجِعُ إِلَى الْمُفْرَدِ إِمَّا مِنْ جِهَةِ وَضْعِهِ وَذَاتِهِ مِثْلَ الِاشْتِرَاكِ وَالْحَقِيقَةِ وَالْمَجَازِ، وَإِمَّا مِنْ جِهَةِ صُورَتِهِ الْإِعْلَالِيَّةِ مِثْلَ «مُخْتَار» اسْمُ فَاعِلٍ وَمَفْعُولٍ أَوِ الْإِدْغَامِيَّةِ مِثْلَ «مُدَّ» مَاضِيًا مَجْهُولًا وَأَمْرًا حَاضِرًا، إِمَّا مِنْ جِهَةِ إِعْرَابِهِ مِثْلَ الْمَرْفُوعِ بِالْمَرْفُوعِ أَوْ مِنْ جِهَةِ إِعْجَامِهِ مِثْلَ الْمُصَحَّفَاتِ.

as poorly constructed sentences. For example, consider the sentence: "Everything that an intelligent person conceptualises is as they have conceived it." Here, we see that the pronoun has the capacity of returning to the active participle or the passive participle. Mistaken understanding may also be caused by perceiving a single term as a compound word, or vice versa.

Regarding errors in meaning, they may relate to the meaning of the preposition, either in the subject, the predicate, or both. This occurs when something is included in the subject or the predicate which is not part of it, and is known as an incorrect syllogism. For example, one may take something which is an accident, and replace it with the subject or the predicate. This is known as the fallacy of misplaced accident.

The next category of errors is those that occur in the meaning of prepositions, and consists of mistakes which may or may not relate to syllogism. An example of a non-syllogism mistake can be seen in posing multiple prepositions within a single preposition, known as a pact or complex preposition. For example, the statement "Zayd is the only writer" appears to be a single preposition, while it is in fact two. The first is to affirm the skill of writing for Zayd, and the second is to negate that skill to anyone besides him.

The fallacies that relate to syllogism will either be in regard to the forms of the preposition, or to its subject and predicate. Another type of fallacy is known as sophistry or begging the question, which is to assume that which you are setting out to prove, smuggling the conclusion into the premise itself.

The fallacy relating to the form of the preposition occurs when one assumes the form to be valid, when it is in fact invalid due to an absence of some of the required conditions. This is known as incorrect composition. In relation to the correct conclusions of the preposition, fallacies exist when the conclusion itself is one of the parts of the preposition, subject, or predicate, known as *muṣādarah*. If the acquired conclusion was not

وَمِنْهُ مَا يَرْجِعُ إِلَى الْمُرَكَّبِ إِمَّا مِنْ جِهَةِ التَّرْكِيبِ نَفْسِهِ كَمَا إِذَا قُلْنَا: «كُلُّ مَا يَتَصَوَّرُهُ الْعَاقِلُ فَهُوَ كَمَا يَتَصَوَّرُهُ» فَيَحْتَمِلُ ضَمِيرُ «هُوَ» أَنْ يَرْجِعَ إِلَى الْعَاقِلِ أَوِ الْمَعْقُولِ. وَإِمَّا مِنْ جِهَةِ أَنْ يُظَنَّ مَا هُوَ الْمُفْرَدُ فِي الْحَقِيقَةِ مُرَكَّبًا أَوْ بِالْعَكْسِ.

وَمِنَ الْمَعْنَوِيِّ مَا يَرْجِعُ إِلَى مَعْنَى الْقَضِيَّةِ إِمَّا مِنْ جِهَةِ جُزْأَيْهَا جَمِيعًا - أَيِ الْمَوْضُوعِ وَالْمَحْمُولِ مِمَّا هُوَ دَاخِلٌ فِيهِ - أَوْ يُعْتَبَرُ فِيهِ مَا لَيْسَ مِنْهُ وَيُقَالُ لِكُلِّ وَاحِدٍ مِنْهُمَا «سُوءُ اعْتِبَارِ الْحَمْلِ». وَمِثْلُ أَنْ يُؤْخَذَ بَدَلَ الْمَوْضُوعِ أَوِ الْمَحْمُولِ مَا هُوَ مِنْ عَوَارِضِهِ أَوْ مَعْرُوضَاتِهِ وَيُقَالُ لِهَذَا: «أَخْذُ مَا بِالْعَرَضِ بَدَلَ مَا بِالذَّاتِ» أَوْ بِالْعَكْسِ أَعْنِي «أَخْذَ مَا بِالذَّاتِ مَكَانَ مَا بِالْعَرَضِ».

وَمِنْهُ مَا يَرْجِعُ إِلَى مَعْنَى الْمُرَكَّبِ مِنَ الْقَضَايَا قِيَاسَاكَاتَ أَوْ غَيْرَ قِيَاسٍ. أَمَّا الَّذِي يَرْجِعُ إِلَى مَعْنَى الْمُرَكَّبِ عَلَى الْقِيَاسِ فَيُقَالُ لَهُ: «إِدْخَالُ مَسَائِلَ فِي مَسْأَلَةٍ» مِثْلَ أَنْ يُقَالَ: «زَيْدٌ كَاتِبٌ وَحْدَهُ» وَيُظَنُّ أَنَّهُ قَضِيَّةٌ وَاحِدَةٌ مَعَ أَنَّهُ مُشْتَمِلٌ عَلَى قَضِيَّتَيْنِ إِحْدَاهُمَا تَثْبُتُ فِيهَا الْكِتَابَةُ لِزَيْدٍ وَالْأُخْرَى تُسْلَبُ فِيهَا الْكِتَابَةُ عَمَّا عَدَاهُ.

وَأَمَّا الَّذِي يَرْجِعُ إِلَى مَعْنَى الْقِيَاسِ إِمَّا مِنْ جِهَةِ مَادَّتِهِ بِأَنْ تَكُونَ شَبِيهَةً بِالْيَقِينِيَّاتِ وَلَيْسَتْ مِنْهَا أَوْ بِالْمُسَلَّمَاتِ وَلَيْسَتْ مِنْهَا فَيُقَالُ لِهَذَا: «سَفْسَطَةٌ» وَ «مُشَاغَبَةٌ». وَإِمَّا مِنْ جِهَةِ صُورَتِهِ بِأَنْ تُرَى صَحِيحَةً وَهِيَ فَاسِدَةٌ حَقِيقَةً لِفَوَاتِ بَعْضِ شُرُوطِهَا وَيُقَالُ لَهُ: «سُوءُ التَّأْلِيفِ» وَ «التَّبْكِيتُ» أَيْضًا. وَإِمَّا مِنْ جِهَةِ نِسْبَتِهِ إِلَى النَّتِيجَةِ مِثْلَ أَنْ تَكُونَ النَّتِيجَةُ عَيْنَ إِحْدَى الْمُقَدِّمَتَيْنِ أَوْ جُزْأَهَا وَيُقَالُ لَهُ: «مُصَادَرَةٌ» وَمِثْلَ

sought after, it is known as an irrelevant conclusion or *ignoratio elenchi*. It is a form of circular reasoning, and is also referred to as placing that which is not a cause as a cause. These are the well-known errors and mistakes in acquiring knowledge, so the student should learn them so as to protect themselves from falling into error.

It is also necessary to beware of those mistakes which afflict intelligent students. These mistakes normally fall into one of two issues, or a combination of both. The first is reading a text too quickly, whereas the second is constantly digressing from one subject to the next. As for reading too quickly, when one's mind is accustomed to excessively fast reading it becomes incapable of organising the knowledge learnt or differentiating between various types of information. Thus, the information learnt is confused and unorganised, like the dreams of sleepers. When one poses questions to such a person, they are incapable of providing an answer because all of the information has not been given a proper form or order. Thus, such a person is incapable of expressing and explaining the knowledge they have learnt.

The second error is that of digressing from one thing to the next, and is harmful because the one who does so will become accustomed to minimal attention. He or she will constantly move from one idea to the next, even with only the smallest amount of association between the two ideas, failing to take into regard the true benefit of the original topic. Due to this, one is distanced from what they originally sought to obtain gradually, stage by stage. Thereafter, one does not have the ability to go back to the original subject, and, if they attempt to do so, they will not be able to identify the train of thought that led to the initial progression of ideas. Such a person becomes more and more misguided and confused. We find them continuously drifting from one state of confusion to the next, and if they persist in this state they will become from among the people of

أَنْ تَكُونَ النَّتِيجَةُ الْمُسْتَفَادَةُ غَيْرَ مَطْلُوبَةٍ وَيُقَالُ لَهُ: «وَضْعُ مَا لَيْسَ بِعِلَّةٍ عِلَّةً». هَذِهِ هِيَ الْأَسْبَابُ الْمَشْهُورَةُ لِلْغَلَطِ فَيَجِبُ أَنْ يَسْتَحْضِرَهَا الطَّالِبُ لِلتَّوَقِّي وَالِاحْتِرَازِ عَنْهَا.

وَيَنْبَغِي لِكُلِّ طَالِبٍ أَنْ يَحْتَرِزَ مِنَ الْوَرْطَةِ الَّتِي يَقَعُ فِيهَا غَالِبُ الْأَذْكِيَاءِ وَإِنَّمَا يَقَعُ فِيهَا مَنْ يَقَعُ بِأَحَدِ أَمْرَيْنِ أَوْ بِهِمَا جَمِيعًا. أَحَدُهُمَا: أَنْ يُعَوِّدَ فِكْرَهُ بِفَرْطِ السُّرْعَةِ. وَالْآخَرُ: أَنْ يَتَّبِعَ كُلَّ سَانِحٍ. أَمَّا الْأَوَّلُ؛ فَلِأَنَّ الْمُفَكِّرَةَ إِذَا اعْتَادَتْ بِإِفْرَاطِ السُّرْعَةِ فِي حَرَكَتِهَا عَجَزَ الذِّهْنُ عَنْ تَرْتِيبِ الْمُسْتَحْضَرَاتِ وَعَنْ تَمْيِيزِ بَعْضِهَا عَنْ بَعْضٍ حَقَّ التَّمْيِيزِ فَتَكُونُ الْمَعَانِي الْمُسْتَحْضَرَةُ أَخْلَاطًا غَيْرَ مُتَرَتِّبَةٍ مِثْلَ أَضْغَاثِ أَحْلَامِ النَّائِمِ فَإِذَا طُولِبَ بِالْمَآلِ وَالْمُحَصَّلِ عَجَزَ عَنِ الْجَوَابِ؛ لِأَنَّ تِلْكَ الْكَثْرَةَ لَمْ تَلْبَسْ لِبَاسًا وَحْدَانِيًّا وَلَمْ تُفَضْ عَلَيْهَا صُورَةُ الْوَحْدَةِ بِسَبَبِ التَّرْتِيبِ حَتَّى يُعَبَّرَ عَنْهَا.

وَأَمَّا الثَّانِي؛ فَلِأَنَّهُ إِذَا اعْتَادَهُ بِاتِّبَاعِ كُلِّ سَانِحٍ لَا يَزَالُ يُسْنَحُ لَهُ مِنْ كُلِّ سَانِحٍ سَانِحٌ آخَرُ بِأَدْنَى مُلَابَسَةٍ بَيْنَهُمَا سَوَاءٌ كَانَ لَهُ مَسَاسٌ بِالْمَقَامِ أَوْ لَا، فَيَبْعُدُ بِذَلِكَ عَنِ الْمَقْصُودِ بِمَرَاحِلَ وَلَا يَقْدِرُ عَلَى الرُّجُوعِ إِلَيْهِ. وَإِنْ رَجَعَ لَا يَجُدُ الطَّرِيقَ إِلَيْهِ فَيَزْدَادُ ضَلَالًا وَمَا زَالَ يَنْتَقِلُ مِنْ نَاقِصٍ إِلَى نَاقِصٍ وَمِنْ ضَلَالٍ إِلَى ضَلَالٍ.

compounded ignorance. This group considers their knowledge to be deep and intricate: if they are asked for some conclusive outcome or for any information, they will say, "The answer to this is very complex and not everyone can understand it", or a similar statement.

As for the one who has been afflicted with this, is aware of its danger and wants to rid themselves of the problem, they must be constantly mindful of their hastiness in study. They must demand from themselves a summary and outcome for every question or topic they have studied, regardless of how short or long it is. They should not proceed forward until they have solidified that summary in their mind completely, and have made that summary the base that everything that follows is built upon. Thereafter, they should build upon that base, being mindful not to stray too far away from that foundation. Everything that he or she learns secondarily connected to the foundation will add to that base and, when they study it again, the foundation and the new information should create a more complete form than the original. They should then study the connection between the two forms that they have just conceptualised and should not progress beyond the secondary information until they have firmly understood the link between it and the first. They should not digress before completing this part of their study by investigating other topics, as doing so before firmly grasping the initial subject will make one incapable of solidifying and understanding the information comprehensively. This will stretch the meaning of what has previously been learnt in a way that will cause disorder and a lack of organisation.

The researcher or student should not be hasty in their study. They should not move forward from one topic to the next before firmly establishing the first, nor should they move from one chapter to the next, or from one science to the next, until they have gained mastery in the original area. The primary

فَإِنِ اسْتَقَرَّ وَأَصَرَّ عَلَى ذَلِكَ كَانَ مِنَ الْمُحَرِّرِينَ الَّذِينَ هُمْ أَصْحَابُ الْجَهْلِ الْمُرَكَّبِ وَهُمْ يَعُدُّونَ ذَلِكَ تَدْقِيقًا وَتَحْقِيقًا، فَإِذَا طُولِبُوا بِالنَّتِيجَةِ يَقُولُونَ: هَذَا مَعْنًى دَقِيقٌ لَا يَفْهَمُهُ كُلُّ أَحَدٍ وَمِثْلُ ذَلِكَ مِنَ التُّرَّهَاتِ.

وَأَمَّا مَنِ ابْتُلِيَ بِهِ وَتَفَطَّنَ لِقُبْحِهِ وَطَلَبَ الْخَلَاصَ مِنْهُ فَعَلَيْهِ الْمُوَاظَبَةُ عَلَى تَرْكِ الْعَجَلَةِ فِي مُلَاحَظَاتِهَا وَأَنْ يُطَالِبَ نَفْسَهُ بِالْمَآلِ وَالْمُحَصَّلِ فِي كُلِّ مَسْأَلَةٍ وَمَبْحَثٍ كَانَتْ قَصِيرًا أَوْ طَوِيلًا وَلَا يَتَجَاوَزُ عَنْهُ مَا لَمْ يَتَمَكَّنْ هُوَ فِي ذِهْنِهِ غَايَةَ التَّمَكُّنِ. وَيَجْعَلُ خُلَاصَةَ كُلِّ مَبْحَثٍ أَصْلًا وَأَسَاسًا ثُمَّ يَبْنِي عَلَيْهِ مَا يُبْنَى وَلَا يَبْعُدُ عَنْهُ كُلَّ الْبُعْدِ وَكُلَّمَا بَنَى عَلَيْهِ شَيْئًا لَاحَظَهُ ثَانِيًا مَعَ مَا ضُمَّ إِلَيْهِ وَبَنَى عَلَيْهِ ثُمَّ ثُمَّ...

وَفِي كُلِّ مُلَاحَظَةٍ مَعَ ضَمِيمَةٍ يَحْصُلُ لَهُ صُورَةٌ جَدِيدَةٌ غَيْرَ الْأُولَى فَيُلَاحِظُ الِارْتِبَاطَ بَيْنَ الصُّورَتَيْنِ وَلَا يَتَجَاوَزُ إِلَى فُرُوعِ الْفَرْعِ حَتَّى يَضْبِطَ فُرُوعَ الْأَصْلِ. وَلَا يُشَعِّبُ الْكَلَامَ تَشْعِيبًا يَعْجِزُ بِهِ عَنِ الضَّبْطِ وَالْإِحَاطَةِ وَيَنْتَشِرُ بِهِ الْمَعْنَى وَمُخْرِجُهُ عَنْ حَدِّ النِّظَامِ وَالِانْتِظَامِ.

وَيَنْبَغِي لِلْمُطَالِعِ أَنْ لَا يَتَعَجَّلَ فِي مُطَالَعَتِهِ وَلَا يَتَجَاوَزَ عَنْ مَسْأَلَةٍ إِلَى أُخْرَى قَبْلَ إِتْقَانِ الْأُولَى وَلَا مِنْ بَابٍ إِلَى آخَرَ وَلَا مِنْ عِلْمٍ إِلَى آخَرَ حَتَّى يُحَصِّلَ الْمَلَكَةَ فِي الْأُولَى. وَالسَّبَبُ غَالِبًا لِحِرْمَانِ طَالِبِ الْكَمَالِ

cause for students failing to reach perfection is hastiness and impatience. The secondary cause is the desire to learn a book or a type of knowledge for which they are not sufficiently prepared. This may be due to one's desire to raise their status in the sight of people and to gain their acceptance. However, it is impossible that attaining the level of knowledge retention in those sciences for which one is prepared will be a waste of time or deprive the learner from perfection. True perfection is attained by strengthening the knowledge that one possesses, not by an artificial study of books or reading with teachers without proper understanding.

One should not become accustomed to mere memorisation of words and expressions without comprehending their meanings. This type of retention will cause ignorance or stupidity. Researchers have explained that any mental faculty that is abundantly overused to the neglect of other faculties will be strengthened, while the others will weaken and diminish. These neglected faculties will thereafter become dormant, and the effects shall be made apparent. The purpose of study can never be obtained except by thinking and strengthening this ability. When memorisation is strengthened, the ability to think is weakened, except, of course, if one's intention is to memorise some terminologies in order to reflect and ponder their meanings without being overly preoccupied by the words alone.

One should also take care to avoid becoming accustomed to a superficial, shallow reading which prevents deep thinking. This can cause a student to become a shallow scholar, a mere storyteller. It is for this reason that students were prevented from studying books of literature and looking in the books of stories. They were also prevented from presenting to themselves secondary issues aside from the primary issues and proofs, because busying oneself with these issues can cause great harm to the student. The first result of this particular mistake, as

عَنِ الْوُصُولِ إِلَيْهِ هُوَ الْعَجَلَةُ وَتَرْكُ الصَّبْرِ وَالتَّأَنِّي فِي الْقَصِيدِ. وَكَذَا الرَّغْبَةُ فِي مُطَالَعَةِ عِلْمٍ أَوْ كِتَابٍ لَيْسَ لَهُ اسْتِعْدَادٌ قَرِيبٌ بِالنِّسْبَةِ إِلَى ذَلِكَ الْعِلْمِ وَالْكِتَابِ.

وَالْبَاعِثُ عَلَى ذَلِكَ غَالِبًا طَلَبُ التَّرَفُّعِ عِنْدَ النَّاسِ وَطَلَبُ إِقْبَالِهِمْ عَلَيْهِ وَاسْتِحْضَارُ الْمَعْلُومِ الَّتِي لَهُ اسْتِعْدَادٌ قَرِيبٌ بِالنِّسْبَةِ إِلَيْهَا فَلَا يُتَصَوَّرُ أَنَّ هَذَا الْفِعْلَ مِنْهُ يَقْتَضِي حِرْمَانَهُ عَنِ الْكَمَالِ وَيُوجِبُ كَوْنَ سَعْيِهِ عَبَثًا وَضَلَالًا؛ إِذِ الْكَمَالُ الْمَطْلُوبُ إِنَّمَا يَحْصُلُ بِحُصُولِ الْعُلُومِ الْوَاقِعِيَّةِ فِي النَّفْسِ مَضْبُوطَةً حَاضِرَةً عِنْدَهَا، لَا بِإِتْمَامِ الْكُتُبِ بِالْمُطَالَعَةِ السَّطْحِيَّةِ أَوْ بِمُجَرَّدِ قِرَاءَتِهَا الْحَشْوِيَّةِ عَلَى أُسْتَاذٍ بِدُونِ أَنْ يَفْهَمَ مَعَانِيَهَا حَقَّ الْفَهْمِ وَيَمْلِكَهَا مِلْكًا صَحِيحًا.

وَيَنْبَغِي لَهُ أَنْ لَا يَعْتَادَ بِحِفْظِ الْأَلْفَاظِ وَالْعِبَارَاتِ بِدُونِ فَهْمِ مَعَانِيهَا؛ لِأَنَّ مِثْلَ هَذَا الْحِفْظِ يُورِثُ الْبَلَادَةَ، بِنَاءً عَلَى أَنَّ الْمُحَقِّقِينَ قَدْ بَيَّنُوا فِي مَحَلِّهِ أَنَّ أَيَّ قُوَّةٍ مِنْ قُوَى الدِّمَاغِيَّةِ اسْتُعْمِلَ كَثِيرًا زَائِدًا عَلَى اسْتِعْمَالِ مَا عَدَاهَا قَوِيَتْ تِلْكَ الْقُوَّةُ وَضَعُفَتْ مَا عَدَاهَا وَتَقَاعَدَتْ عَنْ حَرَكَتِهَا وَإِظْهَارِ مَا فِي وُسْعِهَا مِنَ الْآثَارِ.

وَمَقْصُودُ الْمُطَالِعِ لَا يَتَحَاصَلُ إِلَّا بِإِعْمَالِ الْمُفَكِّرَةِ وَقُوَّتِهَا فَإِذَا قَوِيَتِ الْحَافِظَةُ ضَعُفَتِ الْمُفَكِّرَةُ إِلَّا أَنْ يَكُونَ مُرَادُهُ مِنْ حِفْظِ بَعْضِ الْعِبَارَاتِ اسْتِدَامَةَ الْمُلَاحَظَةِ فِيهَا وَالتَّأَمُّلَ فِي مَعَانِيهَا بِلَا تَشْوِيشِ النَّظَرِ فِي النُّقُوشِ. وَيَنْبَغِي لَهُ أَنْ لَا يَعْتَادَ بِالنَّظَرِ الْإِجْمَالِيِّ السَّطْحِيِّ الَّذِي لَا يَقْتَضِيهِ إِمْعَانُ النَّظَرِ وَتَدْقِيقُهُ؛ فَإِنَّهُ يُوجِبُ كَوْنَهُ حَشْوِيًّا ظَاهِرِيًّا مِثْلَ الْقَصَّاصِينَ.

mentioned, is that one becomes a superficial scholar without the ability to think deeply. The second outcome is pride and arrogance stemming from the general public's desire for this type of knowledge. This is in fact more harmful than the first.

However, an initial reading followed by a deeper reading and careful inspection is one of the necessary etiquettes of studying. Going into detail and depth after a general introduction makes knowledge settle more firmly. One must not accustom their mind to ease and comfort. Rather, they must exercise their mind and keep it moving and active for the majority of the time by keeping it busy with intricate topics and resolving complex questions. This is necessary because when the mind becomes accustomed to idleness it is initially a thing of choice. However, it will eventually lead to a compelled, irresistible state of idleness, which ultimately causes stupidity and ignorance.

A student must also avoid constantly relying on commentaries, marginal notes, or other writings to explain things because he or she is incapable of understanding the topic concerned. Rather, the student should persistently study the written works until he or she has figured it out for themselves, or until they have given up all hope. Thereafter, they should refer to the books of commentary and explanation to compare what was derived with the books of commentary and the marginal notes. One may also compare their own understanding to that which their teacher has derived from the work in order to find out that which they were completely incapable of figuring out on their own. However, before reaching that final point of incapacity, there is great harm caused by giving up on thinking and familiarising the mind with inactivity. One must also forgo reading and studying when they see signs of boredom due to any of its causes. This is because the mind makes many mistakes when it is bored.

One should also refrain or desist from studying when their mind is busy with thoughts and different ideas that cause a

وَكَذَا يَمْنَعُ الطَّالِبَ قَبْلَ الرُّسُوخِ وَالْكَمَالِ عَنْ مُطَالَعَةِ الْكُتُبِ الْأَدَبِيَّةِ وَعَنِ النَّظَرِ فِي كُتُبِ الْمُحَاضَرَاتِ وَعَنِ الِاشْتِغَالِ بِالْفُرُوعِ الْمُجَرَّدَةِ عَنِ الْأُصُولِ وَالدَّلَائِلِ؛ لِأَنَّ فِي الِاشْتِغَالِ بِهَا ضَرَرَيْنِ عَظِيمَيْنِ فِي حَقِّ الطَّالِبِ أَحَدُهُمَا: مَا ذَكَرْنَا مِنْ كَوْنِهِ حَشْوِيًّا ظَاهِرِيًّا غَيْرَ قَادِرٍ عَلَى التَّحْقِيقِ. وَالْآخَرُ: هُوَ الْعُجْبُ بِسَبَبِ رَغْبَةِ الْعَوَامِّ فِيهِ وَاعْتِنَاءِ الْجَهَلَةِ بِهِ، وَهَذَا فِي الْحَقِيقَةِ أَضَرُّ مِنَ الْأَوَّلِ. وَأَمَّا النَّظَرُ الْإِجْمَالِيُّ الَّذِي يَعْقُبُهُ تَعْمِيقُ النَّظَرِ وَالْإِمْعَانُ فَهُوَ مِنْ جُمْلَةِ الْآدَابِ الْوَاجِبَةِ الْمُرَاعَاةِ؛ لِأَنَّ التَّفْصِيلَ بَعْدَ الْإِجْمَالِ أَوْقَعُ شَيْءٍ فِي النُّفُوسِ.

وَيَنْبَغِي أَنْ لَا يُعَوِّدَ فِكْرَهُ بِالدَّعَةِ وَالرَّاحَةِ؛ بَلْ يُرَوِّضُهُ وَيُحَرِّكُهُ فِي أَغْلَبِ الْأَوْقَاتِ بِأَنْ يَسْتَعْمِلَهُ فِي الْمَبَاحِثِ الدَّقِيقَةِ وَالْمَسَائِلِ الْعَمِيقَةِ؛ لِأَنَّ الْمُفَكِّرَةَ إِذَا اعْتَادَتْ بِالسُّكُونِ أَدَّى هَذَا السُّكُونُ الِاخْتِيَارِيُّ فِي أَوَّلِهِ إِلَى السُّكُونِ الِاضْطِرَارِيِّ فِي آخِرِهِ، وَهُوَ يُوجِبُ الْبَلَادَةَ وَالْغَبَاوَةَ؛ لِأَنَّ مَحَلَّ الْمُفَكِّرَةِ عَلَى مَا بَيَّنَ فِي مَحَلِّهِ هُوَ التَّجْوِيفُ الْأَوْسَطُ مِنَ الدِّمَاغِ فَإِذَا سَكَنَتْ وَتَقَاعَدَتْ عَنِ الْحَرَكَةِ زَمَانًا مَدِيدًا امْتَلَأَ ذَلِكَ الْمَحَلُّ بِالْبُخَارِ الْكَدِرِ الْغَلِيظِ بِحَيْثُ تَعْجِزُ الْمُفَكِّرَةُ عَنْ حَرَكَةٍ عِنْدَ إِرَادَةِ الْحَرَكَةِ، إِذَا كَثُرَ وَكَثُفَ ذَلِكَ الْبُخَارُ فَتَقَاعَدَتِ الْمُفَكِّرَةُ اضْطِرَارًا إِمَّا بِالْكُلِّيَّةِ أَوْ عَنِ الْحَرَكَةِ الْمُعْتَدِلَةِ النَّافِعَةِ فِي تَحْصِيلِ الْمَطْلُوبِ بِهَا.

وَيَنْبَغِي لَهُ أَنْ لَا يَتَعَجَّلَ إِلَى الْمُرَاجَعَةِ إِلَى الشُّرُوحِ أَوْ إِلَى الْحَوَاشِي أَوِ التَّحْرِيرَاتِ إِذَا عَجَزَ فِي الْجُمْلَةِ عَنِ اسْتِخْرَاجِ الْمَحَلِّ؛ بَلْ يُلَاحِظُهُ وَقْتًا بَعْدَ وَقْتٍ حَتَّى يَظْهَرَ عَلَيْهِ آثَارُ الْمَقْصُودِ أَوِ الْعَجْزُ التَّامُّ عَنْ دَرَكِهِ ثُمَّ يُرَاجِعُ إِلَى مَا يُرَاجِعُ إِمَّا لِتَطْبِيقِ مُسْتَخْرِجِهِ عَلَى مَا فِي الشُّرُوحِ وَالْحَوَاشِي أَوْ عَلَى مُسْتَخْرَجِ أُسْتَاذِهِ وَإِمَّا لِلِاسْتِدْلَالِ عِنْدَ ظُهُورِ الْعَجْزِ التَّامِّ. وَأَمَّا قَبْلَ

distraction. One should also refrain or desist from studying at the time of hunger or when one is completely satiated, as well as when one is thirsty or excessively tired. Each of these states will cloud the mind and dull its ability to think. For indeed, studying depends on focusing one's thoughts and mind, as this leads to excellent understanding. It is necessary to take into consideration these things and protect from that which goes against studying. It is for this reason that they say one should choose a time for studying that will be the best for focusing thoughts, having a clear mind, and strong thinking; for example during the last third of the night.

One must be aware of not boldly entering into a debate before having studied sufficiently, even if it is a topic which is clear to the person. Indeed, debate and discussion before studying does not produce anything except for loss and regret. Rather, before debating, one should not be satisfied with that which was solely understood from individual *muṭālaʿah* and their own opinion. One should present their understanding to others, either by studying or discussing it with those whom they trust from their friends, or by reviewing it with their teacher. That which is known through group study is much more comprehensive than that which became clear through individual study. Group study is an activity of multiple minds, while studying in solitude is an activity of one mind alone: the individual seldom gains a benefit equal to that which is attained by an entire group.

One should also hold a good opinion of their contemporaries and the pious predecessors. They should not look down on anyone regarding their speech or understanding, and should instead hold a sceptical opinion of one's self. They must be very careful to not become deluded by their own understanding and mental acumen as this will lead to him or her to refrain from seeking out knowledge and participating in its gatherings. The student will thus rely solely on their own ability to study the

ذَلِكَ أَعْنِي عِنْدَ الْعَجْزِ فِي الْجُمْلَةِ فَفِي الْمُرَاجَعَةِ ضَرَرٌ مِثْلُ ضَرَرِ تَرْكِ الْفِكْرِ عَلَى حَالِهِ وَتَعْوِيدِهِ بِالسُّكُوتِ.

وَيَنْبَغِي لَهُ أَنْ يَتْرُكَ الْمُطَالَعَةَ عِنْدَ ظُهُورِ الْكَلَالِ وَالْمَلَالِ بِسَبَبٍ مِنَ الْأَسْبَابِ؛ لِأَنَّ الذِّهْنَ إِذَا كَلَّ وَمَلَّ أَخْطَأَ كَثِيرًا. وَأَنْ يَتْرُكَهَا أَيْضًا عِنْدَ اشْتِغَالِ الْبَالِ بِبَعْضِ الْخَوَاطِرِ الضَّرُورِيَّةِ وَبِبَعْضِ الْحِسِّيَّاتِ وَالْوَهْمِيَّاتِ وَعِنْدَ تَفَرُّقِهِ وَتَشَتُّتِهِ بِبَعْضِ الْمَذْكُورَاتِ وَعِنْدَ الشِّبَعِ وَالْجُوعِ وَالْعَطَشِ وَالسَّهَرِ الْمُفْرِطِ؛ لِأَنَّ كُلَّ وَاحِدٍ مِنْهَا مُشَوِّشٌ لِلذِّهْنِ وَمُفَرِّقٌ لِلْبَالِ.

وَالْمَدَارُ فِي الْمُطَالَعَةِ عَلَى جَمْعِيَّةِ الْخَاطِرِ وَصَفَاءِ الذِّهْنِ وَجَوْدَةِ الْفَهْمِ فَيَجِبُ مُرَاعَاتُهَا وَالِاحْتِرَازُ عَمَّا يُضَادُّهَا؛ وَلِذَلِكَ قَالُوا: يَنْبَغِي أَنْ يُخْتَارَ لِلْمُطَالَعَةِ وَقْتًا يَكُونُ فِيهِ جَمْعِيَّةُ الْخَاطِرِ وَصَفَاءُ الذِّهْنِ وَقُوَّةُ الْفِكْرِ أَزْيَدَ مِنْ سَائِرِ الْأَوْقَاتِ مِثْلَ الثُّلُثِ الْأَخِيرِ مِنَ اللَّيْلِ؛ فَإِنَّهُ أَجْمَعُ لِلْأُمُورِ الْمَذْكُورَةِ مِنْ غَيْرِهِ.

وَيَنْبَغِي لَهُ أَنْ لَا يَتَجَاسَرَ عَلَى الْمُنَاظَرَةِ قَبْلَ الْمُطَالَعَةِ وَإِنْ كَانَ الْمَحَلُّ عِنْدَهُ أَظْهَرَ مَا يَكُونُ؛ فَإِنَّ الْمُنَاظَرَةَ قَبْلَ الْمُطَالَعَةِ لَا تُثْمِرُ غَالِبًا سِوَى الْخَجَالَةِ وَالنَّدَامَةِ. وَأَنْ لَا يُصِرَّ عَلَى مَا اسْتَقَرَّ عَلَيْهِ رَأْيُهُ وَتَمَكَّنَ فِيهِ فِكْرُهُ عِنْدَ الْمُطَالَعَةِ قَبْلَ عَرْضِهِ إِمَّا بِطَرِيقِ الْمُذَاكَرَةِ عَلَى مَنْ يَثِقُ بِنُهْيِهِ مِنْ أَقْرَانِهِ أَوْ بِطَرِيقِ الْمُدَارَسَةِ أَوْ أُسْتَاذِهِ؛ فَإِنَّ الْغَالِبَ أَنْ يَظْهَرَ بِالْمُذَاكَرَةِ مَا لَا يَظْهَرُ بِالْمُطَالَعَةِ؛ إِذِ الْمُذَاكَرَةُ بِتَعَاوُنِ الْعُقُولِ وَالْمُطَالَعَةُ بِعَقْلٍ وَاحِدٍ وَالْمُنْفَرِدُ لَا يُدْرِكُ فَضِيلَةَ الْجَمَاعَةِ.

وَيَنْبَغِي لَهُ أَنْ يُحْسِنَ ظَنَّهُ فِي حَقِّ السَّلَفِ وَالْخَلَفِ وَلَا يَسْتَحْقِرَ أَحَدًا فِي قَوْلِهِ وَفَهْمِهِ وَيُسِيءَ الظَّنَّ فِي نَفْسِهِ. وَيَجِبُ عَلَيْهِ أَنْ يَحْتَرِزَ كُلَّ

topics in which they feel prepared, placing complete trust in their own memory. Beware of this; forgetfulness is a necessary accident of human beings. Lastly, one must take absolute care to avoid bad manners in regard to one's pious predecessors, because this is a major cause of deprivation of reaching perfection. We ask Allah for His noble enablement and for good manners with our pious predecessors and our peers at all times.

الِاحْتِرَازِ عَنْ أَنْ يَغْتَرَّ بِفَهْمِهِ وَذَكَائِهِ فَيَتْرُكَ الطَّلَبَ وَمَجَالِسَ الْأَسَاتِيذِ، وَيُكَرِّرَ الْمُطَالَعَةَ فِي مَبَاحِثَ لَهُ اسْتِحْضَارُ اعْتِمَادًا عَلَى ضَبْطِهِ وَحِفْظِهِ إِيَّاهَا؛ إِذِ النِّسْيَانُ مِنْ لَوَازِمِ الْبَشَرِ وَيَحْتَرِزَ غَايَةَ الِاحْتِرَازِ عَنْ إِسَاءَةِ الْأَدَبِ فِي حَقِّ السَّلَفِ؛ فَإِنَّهُ مُوجِبٌ قَوِيٌّ لِلْحِرْمَانِ عَنِ الْكَمَالِ، نَسْأَلُ اللهَ التَّوْفِيقَ عَلَى حِفْظِ الْآدَابِ مَعَ السَّلَفِ وَالْخَلَفِ فِي كُلِّ حَالٍ.

$$\approx$$

Conclusion
AN EXPLANATION FOR GROUP STUDY AND SOME OF ITS CONDITIONS AND ETIQUETTES

Group study, according to the terminology of researchers, is defined in the exact same manner as debate. The only difference is that group study takes place between two or more parties whose positions are not established, whereas debate is between two defined groups. When debating, one party assumes the position of affirmation and the other party assumes the position of negation. Alternatively, group study consists of each participant taking turns supporting both sides of the argument. Group study often occurs between peers who share similarities and are at a similar level of knowledge, whereas debate takes place between peers, associates, and others.

There is a notion that the difference between group study and debate is that debate refers to meanings, while group study refers to words and terminologies. This notion is incorrect. Our discussion regarding both concepts is through only considering independently-existing meanings, not in terms and the meanings that are derived from terms. As for the definition of debate, it is to deeply investigate the relationship of things from two perspectives in order to clarify and agree upon the truth. This definition is based on a subtlety mentioned in the books of debate.

In practice, debate is an exchange of diverging views between two or more well-researched individuals. It is, of course, necessary to include "an exchange of diverging views" in the definition of both debate and of group discussion. True group discussion is when each individual in the group mentions what they have gained from one perspective, after having individually reviewed or studied using all of one's mental capacities so that the truth may become clear to them. The benefit of group discussion is found when all of its conditions are met and its etiquettes are

الذَّيْلُ

فِي بَيَانِ الْمُذَاكَرَةِ وَبَعْضِ شَرَائِطِهَا وَآدَابِهَا

اعْلَمْ أَنَّ الْمُذَاكَرَةَ فِي اصْطِلَاحِ الْمُحَصِّلِينَ عَلَى مَا يُفْهَمُ مِنْ مَوَارِدِ اسْتِعْمَالِهَا هِيَ الْمُنَاظَرَةُ الِاصْطِلَاحِيَّةُ بِعَيْنِهَا؛ إِلَّا أَنَّ الْمُذَاكَرَةَ تَكُونُ بَيْنَ اثْنَيْنِ فَمَا فَوْقَهَا بِخِلَافِ الْمُنَاظَرَةِ، فَإِنَّهَا تَجْرِي بَيْنَ الشَّخْصَيْنِ فَقَطْ كَمَا هُوَ ظَاهِرٌ مِنْ تَعْرِيفِهَا. وَأَيْضًا أَنَّ الْمُذَاكَرَةَ لَا يَتَعَيَّنُ فِيهَا مَنْصِبُ الِاسْتِدْلَالِ وَلَا مَنْصِبُ السُّؤَالِ لِأَحَدِ الطَّرَفَيْنِ كَمَا يَتَعَيَّنُ فِي الْمُنَاظَرَةِ؛ بَلْ يَتَنَاوَبُ الْكُلُّ فِي كُلِّ وَاحِدٍ مِنَ الْمَنْصِبَيْنِ.

وَأَيْضًا أَنَّ الْمُذَاكَرَةَ تَكُونُ بَيْنَ الْأَقْرَانِ وَالْأَمْثَالِ الْمُتَقَارِبِينَ وَالْمُتَسَاوِينَ فِي الْمَرْتَبَةِ بِخِلَافِ الْمُنَاظَرَةِ؛ فَإِنَّهَا تَعُمُّ الْأَقْرَاتَ وَالْمُتَفَاوِتِينَ. وَأَمَّا الْفَرْقُ بِأَنَّ الْمُنَاظَرَةَ إِنَّمَا تَكُونُ فِي الْمَعْنَى وَالْمُذَاكَرَةُ فِي الْأَلْفَاظِ فَلَيْسَ بِشَيْءٍ، فَإِنَّ كَلَامَنَا فِي الِاصْطِلَاحِيِّ مِنْ كُلٍّ مِنْهُمَا، لَا فِي اللُّغَوِيِّ وَلَا فِي الِاصْطِلَاحِيِّ كُلٌّ مِنْهُمَا يَقَعُ فِي الْمَعْنَى بِوَاسِطَةِ الْأَلْفَاظِ.

وَأَمَّا تَعْرِيفُ الْمُنَاظَرَةِ بِأَنَّهَا هِيَ: «النَّظَرُ بِالْبَصِيرَةِ مِنَ الطَّرَفَيْنِ فِي النِّسْبَةِ بَيْنَ الشَّيْئَيْنِ إِظْهَارًا لِلصَّوَابِ» فَمَبْنِيٌّ عَلَى نُكْتَةٍ كَمَا بَيَّنَ فِي كُتُبِ الْمُنَاظَرَةِ، وَإِلَّا فَحَقِيقَتُهَا هِيَ الْمُدَافَعَةُ بِالْكَلَامِ مِنَ الشَّخْصَيْنِ النَّاظِرَيْنِ بِالْبَصِيرَةِ فِي النِّسْبَةِ بَيْنَ الشَّيْئَيْنِ طَلَبًا لِظُهُورِ الصَّوَابِ. وَكَذَا الْمُذَاكَرَةُ هِيَ الْمُدَافَعَةُ بِالْكَلَامِ مِنَ الشَّخْصَيْنِ النَّاظِرَيْنِ بِالْبَصِيرَةِ أَوْ مِنْ جَمَاعَةٍ نَاظِرِينَ كَذَلِكَ... إلخ.

فَيَجِبُ أَنْ يُقَدَّرَ «الْمُدَافَعَةُ بِالْكَلَامِ» فِي تَعْرِيفِ كُلٍّ وَاحِدٍ مِنَ الْمُنَاظَرَةِ

observed. It is even said that group discussion for one hour is better than reading and studying for a day. In fact, it is better than many days because reading and studying happens with one mind and intellect, whereas group discussion happens with many minds. The benefit of a collective effort over a single person's is self-evident. Similarly, the benefits of group discussion are clear and great in number, not requiring explanation. However, these benefits are based on the adherence to certain conditions and etiquettes. If these conditions are not found and the etiquettes are ignored, then it is better to forgo group study as it will only lead to argumentation and fighting, which causes the truth to be lost.

From the conditions of group study are that the entire group is on the same level as the people of good understanding and clear minds, none wanting to surpass the other or seek leadership over the others. There must not be any fights or argumentation between them, nor any foolishness or light-hearted joking. However, there is no harm if there is someone amongst them who is slow in learning and does not understand things except after much repetition and explanation. This person's affliction does not affect anyone else, unlike the examples mentioned previously which will affect the entire group and prevent the attainment of truth, restricting the benefits of group study and discussion.

Also from the conditions of group study is that the individuals in the group have an affinity for one another, a familiarity amongst themselves, and harbour no hatred nor animosity. Love brings clarity, which in turn brings about an understanding of intent or meaning, just as hatred causes the opposite. Familiarity also necessitates enjoyment and openness, which causes swift understanding, just as unfamiliarity causes close-mindedness, slow understanding, and a lack of clarity.

Another condition of group study is that each individual in the group knows the vernacular of the other, and possess

وَالْمُذَاكَرَةُ فَحَقِيقَةُ الْمُذَاكَرَةِ أَنْ يَذْكُرَ كُلٌّ وَاحِدٍ مِنَ الشَّخْصَيْنِ أَوِ الْجَمَاعَةِ مَا عِنْدَهُ مِمَّا يَتَعَلَّقُ بِنِسْبَةٍ وَاحِدَةٍ بَعْدَ أَنْ يُلاحِظَهَا بِقَدْرِ وُسْعِهِ طَلَبًا لِظُهُورِ مَا هُوَ الْحَقُّ وَالصَّوَابُ. وَنَفْعُ الْمُذَاكَرَةِ عَظِيمٌ إِذَا وُجِدَتْ شَرَائِطُهَا وَرُوعِيَتْ آدَابُهَا، حَتَّى قِيلَ: مُذَاكَرَةُ سَاعَةٍ خَيْرٌ مِنْ مُطَالَعَةِ يَوْمٍ بَلْ أَيَّامٍ؛ لِأَنَّ الْمُطَالَعَةَ بِعَقْلٍ وَاحِدٍ وَالْمُذَاكَرَةَ بِعُقُولٍ، وَفَضِيلَةُ الْجَمَاعَةِ عَلَى الْفَرْدِ أَظْهَرُ مِنْ أَنْ تُخْفَى، وَمَنَافِعُ الْمُذَاكَرَةِ كَثِيرَةٌ بَيِّنَةٌ غَنِيَّةٌ عَنِ الْبَيَانِ؛ إِلَّا أَنَّ هَذِهِ الْمَنَافِعَ إِنَّمَا تَتَرَتَّبُ عَلَيْهَا عِنْدَ وُجُودِ الشَّرَائِطِ وَمُرَاعَاةِ الْآدَابِ. وَإِذَا لَمْ يُوجَدِ الشَّرَائِطُ وَالْآدَابُ فَتَرْكُهَا أَنْفَعُ؛ لِأَنَّهَا حِينَئِذٍ تُؤَدِّي إِلَى الْمِرَاءِ وَاللَّجَاجِ الْمُوجِبَيْنِ لِمَحْقِ الْحَقِّ وَالصَّوَابِ.

وَمِنْ شَرَائِطِهَا: أَنْ تَكُونَ الْجَمَاعَةُ مُنْصِفِينَ ذَوِي الْأَفْهَامِ الْجَيِّدَةِ وَالْأَذْهَانِ الصَّافِيَةِ، لَا يُرِيدُ أَحَدٌ مِنْهُمُ التَّفَوُّقَ عَلَى مَا عَدَاهُ وَلَا يَدَّعِي الرِّيَاسَةَ عَلَيْهِمْ. وَأَنْ لَا يَكُونَ بَيْنَهُمْ لَجُوجٌ مُعَانِدٌ وَلَا سَفِيهٌ مُجَرْبِزٌ وَلَا خَفِيفٌ هُزَالٌ، وَلَا بَأْسَ إِنْ كَانَ فِيهِمْ غَبِيٌّ لَا يَفْهَمُ الْكَلَامَ إِلَّا بِالتَّكْرَارِ وَالتَّفْصِيلِ؛ لِأَنَّ ضَرَرَهُ لَا يَتَعَدَّى إِلَى الْغَيْرِ بِخِلَافِ مَنْ شَرَطْنَا عَدَمَهُ؛ فَإِنَّ ضَرَرَهُ يَعُمُّ الْكُلَّ وَيَمْنَعُ عَنِ الْوُصُولِ إِلَى الْحَقِّ وَعَنْ ظُهُورِ ثَمَرَةِ الْمُذَاكَرَةِ عَلَيْهِمْ.

وَمِنْ شُرُوطِهَا: كَوْنُ الْجَمَاعَةِ مُتَحَابِّينَ وَمُتَوَانِسِينَ لَا مُتَبَاغِضِينَ وَمُتَوَحِّشِينَ؛ لِأَنَّ الْمَحَبَّةَ تُوجِبُ حُسْنَ الْإِصْغَاءِ وَهُوَ يَسْتَلْزِمُ فَهْمَ الْمُرَادِ كَمَا أَنَّ التَّبَاغُضَ يَقْتَضِي خِلَافَ ذَلِكَ وَأَنَّ التَّآنُسَ وَالتَّأَلُّفَ يَقْتَضِي الِانْبِسَاطَ وَهُوَ يُوجِبُ سُرْعَةَ الْفَهْمِ وَجَوْدَتَهُ كَمَا أَنَّ التَّوَحُّشَ يُوجِبُ الِانْقِبَاضَ الْمُوجِبَ لِسُوءِ الْفَهْمِ وَبُطْئِهِ.

وَمِنْ شُرُوطِهَا: أَنْ يَكُونَ كُلُّ وَاحِدٍ مِنَ الْجَمَاعَةِ عَارِفًا بِلَهْجَةِ الْآخَرِ وَاقِفًا

an understanding of their habits of expression. Each person's intent must be clear between the others from the beginning, preventing unwarranted objections to each person's method.

It is incumbent for every wise participant in every group study or debate to avoid taking the position of a claimant who is forced to provide supportive evidence. The one who adopts this position places undue difficulty and hardship upon themselves. Ease and facilitation can be found by questioning and investigation. In fact, the one questioning is in the easiest position and safest from the embarrassment of being silenced. Whoever seeks safety from embarrassment and regret should choose the position of questioning, and not see themselves as the final authoritative word on anything, even if they are in fact the authority in an area due to their research. This is because human beings are never free from regret and mistake. Such a person should portray themselves as a transmitter of knowledge from somebody else, while being doubtful as to what they are presenting to the group. If it is possible, one should hold oneself back from opening the discussion and wait until another opens the door. Then they may take the position of questioning and investigating the other person. However, if one is forced to open the door themselves, they should do so by indicating the general, basic aspects of the topic without any explanation or details. They should then carefully ask, "What do the brothers say or think about this?", using gentle words and articulations with humility. This will incite love and familiarity in the discussion, whatever the topic may be. Thereafter, they should quiet themselves in order to avoid the position of the claimant. However, if someone goes further in questioning and investigation, firmly seeking an explanation from them, then they should answer the questions in a way that does not make any type of claim or necessitate a proof.

One should state everything as a transmitter who is doubtful about that information and is not firm. This way, questions

عَلَى عَادَتِهِ فِي التَّعْبِيرِ لِيَتَّضِحَ مُرَادُ كُلِّ وَاحِدٍ مِنْهُمْ عَلَى الْآخَرِ مِنْ أَوَّلِ الْأَمْرِ فَلَا يُؤَدِّي إِلَى الْمُنَاقَشَةِ فِي التَّعْبِيرِ.

وَمِمَّا يَنْبَغِي لِكُلِّ مُذَاكِرٍ وَمُنَاظِرٍ عَارِفٍ أَنْ يَحْتَرِزَ عَنْ جَلْبِ مَنْصِبِ الدَّعْوَى وَالِاسْتِدْلَالِ إِلَى نَفْسِهِ؛ فَإِنَّ جَمِيعَ الشَّدَائِدِ وَالْمَشَاقِّ فِي ذَلِكَ الْمَنْصِبِ كَمَا أَنَّ السُّهُولَةَ وَالْخِفَّةَ كُلَّهَا فِي مَنْصِبِ السُّؤَالِ وَالِاسْتِفْسَارِ؛ بَلِ الِاسْتِفْسَارُ هُوَ أَسْهَلُ الطُّرُقِ وَأَسْلَمُهَا عَنْ خَجَالَةِ الْإِلْزَامِ وَالْإِفْحَامِ. فَمَنْ يُرِيدُ الْيُسْرَ وَالسَّلَامَةَ عَنِ الْخَجَالَةِ وَالنَّدَامَةِ يَخْتَارُ طَرِيقَ الِاسْتِفْسَارِ فَلَا يُرِي نَفْسَهُ قَاطِعًا فِي شَيْءٍ أَصْلًا وَإِنْ كَانَ قَاطِعًا مُتَيَقِّنًا فِيهِ بِحَسَبِ مُطَالَعَتِهِ؛ لِأَنَّ الْبَشَرَ لَا يَخْلُو عَنِ السَّهْوِ وَالْخَطَأِ، فَيَنْبَغِي لَهُ أَنْ يُظْهِرَ نَفْسَهُ كَأَنَّهُ نَاقِلٌ عَنِ الْغَيْرِ وَهُوَ شَاكٌّ فِيمَا يَعْرِضُهُ عَنِ الْجَمَاعَةِ.

وَإِنْ أَمْكَنَ لَهُ أَنْ يَمْنَعَ نَفْسَهُ عَنِ الْمُبَادَرَةِ إِلَى فَتْحِ بَابِ الْبَحْثِ وَيَتَوَقَّفَ حَتَّى يَفْتَحَهُ الْآخَرُ مِنَ الْجَمَاعَةِ وَيَتَعَيَّنَ لَهُ مَنْصِبُ السُّؤَالِ وَالِاسْتِفْسَارِ. وَإِنِ اضْطُرَّ إِلَى فَتْحِ الْكَلَامِ يَشْرَعُ فِيهِ مُشِيرًا إِلَى أُمِّ الْبَحْثِ وَأَصْلِهِ مُجْمَلًا فِيهِ لَا مُفَصِّلًا وَمُصَرِّحًا بِهِ. فَيَقُولُ: «مَا يَقُولُ الْإِخْوَانُ» أَوْ «مَا رَأْيُكُمْ» أَوْ «مَا يُؤَدِّي مُؤَدَّى ذَلِكَ» بِتَعْبِيرٍ لَطِيفٍ يَشْعُرُ بِالتَّوَاضُعِ وَيُحَرِّكُ عِرْقَ الْمَوَدَّةِ وَالْأُلْفَةِ «فِي الْمَبْحَثِ الْفُلَانِي» ثُمَّ يَسْكُنُ لِيَدْفَعَ عَنْ نَفْسِهِ مَنْصِبَ الدَّعْوَى فَإِذَا فَصَّلَهُ الْآخَرُ بِإِثْرِ السُّؤَالِ وَالِاسْتِفْسَارِ وَإِنْ طَلَبُوا مِنْهُ التَّقْرِيرَ وَالتَّفْصِيلَ الْبَتَّةَ وَجَبَ عَلَيْهِ أَنْ يُقَرِّرَهُ بِوَجْهٍ لَا يَلْتَزِمُ فِيهِ شَيْئًا مِنَ الدَّعْوَى وَالِاسْتِدْلَالِ؛ بَلْ يُقَرِّرُ كُلَّ مَا يُقَدَّرُ كَأَنَّهُ نَاقِلٌ عَنِ الْغَيْرِ وَهُوَ شَاكٌّ فِيهِ غَيْرُ قَاطِعٍ بِحَيْثُ يَتَوَجَّهُ عَلَيْهِ شَيْءٌ مِنَ السُّؤَالِ فَلَا يَحْتَاجُ إِلَى كُلْفَةِ الْجَوَابِ.

cannot be directed at them and they cannot be forced to give conclusive answers. The benefit of having a partner who possesses a comprehensive understanding is equal to the benefit of a good teacher. We used to hear from our teacher ﷺ, that the blessing of studying with a partner who is blessed or has been given noble enablement over studying individually, is like the benefit of *ṣalāh* in *jamāʿah* over *ṣalāh* individually. There is no need for further explanation in this matter.

When a student finds a study partner who is gifted, they must be conscientious of this person's feelings and treat them like a sibling, more carefully than a family member. The student should remain just with them in their group study and discussions. This includes all their dealings in seclusion, in the presence of the teacher, or in the gathering of the class and in the company of people. We have seen many students who act justly during group study, but are reckless in the gatherings of people, abandoning all justice and pursuing a path of reckless severity. Many become unmannered with their teachers when they are in the gatherings attended by laymen. For this reason, the earlier generations of scholars would require students to first cultivate a good internal composition and manners, so that their bad habits do not become a cause for them to be deprived of knowledge and reaching perfection.

WE ASK ALLAH for His enablement for us to observe the etiquettes of seeking knowledge such that we attain their mastery. We praise Him in the beginning and the end, openly and internally, and we send blessings and prayers on our Prophet Muhammad ﷺ, the leader of the first and the last, his family, and companions who fulfilled the etiquettes of his companionship both openly and in secret.

يَنْبَغِي أَنْ يَعْرِفَ أَنَّ مَنْفَعَةَ الشَّرِيكِ الْفَهِيمِ الْمُنْصِفِ الْمُوَافِقِ لَيْسَ بِأَقَلَّ وَأَدْنَى مِنْ مَنْفَعَةِ الْأُسْتَاذِ الْكَامِلِ فِي حَقِّ الطَّالِبِ. وَهَذِهِ الْمَنْفَعَةُ إِنَّمَا تَحْصُلُ بِسَبَبِ الْمُذَاكَرَةِ مَعَهُ. وَقَدْ سَمِعْنَا مِنْ أُسْتَاذِنَا وَسَّعَ اللهُ مَضَاجِعَهُ كَرَّةً بَعْدَ أُخْرَى أَنَّ فَضِيلَةَ الدَّرْسِ مَعَ الشَّرِيكِ الْمُوَافِقِ أَوِ الشُّرَكَاءِ الْمُوَافِقِينَ عَلَى دَرْسِ الْمُنْفَرِدِ كَفَضِيلَةِ صَلَاةِ الْجَمَاعَةِ عَلَى صَلَاةِ الْمُنْفَرِدِ. وَهَذَا ظَاهِرٌ كُلَّ الظُّهُورِ وَلَا يَحْتَاجُ إِلَى الْبَيَانِ.

فَإِذَا وَجَدَ طَالِبٌ شَرِيكًا مُوَافِقًا وَاحِدًا وَمَا فَوْقَهُ يَنْبَغِي أَنْ يُرَاعِيَ خَاطِرَهُ وَيُعَامِلَهُ مُعَامَلَةَ الْأَخِ؛ بَلْ أَشَدَّ مِنْهُمَا، وَأَنْ يُنْصِفَ مَعَهُ فِي مُذَاكَرَتِهِ وَسَائِرِ مُعَامَلَتِهِ فِي الْخَلْوَةِ وَفِي حُضُورِ الْأُسْتَاذِ وَمَجْلِسِ الدَّرْسِ وَفِي حُضُورِ النَّاسِ؛ لِأَنَّا قَدْ رَأَيْنَا كَثِيرًا مِنَ الطَّلَبَةِ يُنْصِفُونَ عِنْدَ الْمُذَاكَرَةِ فِي الْخَلْوَةِ وَيَتَقَشَّفُونَ فِي مَجَالِسِ النَّاسِ وَيَتْرُكُونَ الْإِنْصَافَ وَيَذْهَبُونَ طَرِيقَ الِاعْتِسَافِ؛ بَلْ يُسِيئُونَ الْأَدَبَ مَعَ أُسْتَاذِهِمْ إِذَا كَانَ فِي الْمَجْلِسِ مَنْ يُعْتَدُّ بِهِ مِنَ الْعَوَامِّ.

وَلِذَلِكَ كَانَ الْحُكَمَاءُ الْمُتَقَدِّمُونَ يَأْمُرُونَ الطَّالِبَ أَوَّلًا بِتَهْذِيبِ الْأَخْلَاقِ حَتَّى لَا يَكُونَ سُوءُ الْخُلُقِ سَبَبًا لِإِسَاءَةِ الْأَدَبِ الَّتِي هِيَ سَبَبُ الْحِرْمَانِ عَنِ الْبُلُوغِ إِلَى الْكَمَالِ.

نَسْأَلُ اللهَ التَّوْفِيقَ لِمُرَاعَاةِ الْأَدَبِ فِي طَرِيقِ الطَّلَبِ حَتَّى نَصِلَ بِمُحَافَظَةِ الْأَدَبِ إِلَى الْأَرَبِّ، وَنَحْمَدُهُ فِي الْأَوَّلِ وَالْآخِرِ وَالظَّاهِرِ وَالْبَاطِنِ، وَنُصَلِّي عَلَى نَبِيِّهِ سَيِّدِنَا مُحَمَّدٍ سَيِّدِ الْأَوَّلِ وَالْآخِرِ وَعَلَى آلِهِ وَصَحْبِهِ الْمُتَأَدِّبِينَ بِآدَابِهِ فِي الْبَاطِنِ وَالظَّاهِرِ.

Indeed the pen has rested from inscribing these pages on the third of the third, of the fourth of the third, of the second of the second [3 Rabīʿ al-Awwal 1124 AH]. May Allah send blessings and peace upon our master Muhammad ﷺ, and upon his family and companions.

⬥

The scribe is ʿAbd al-Bārī ibn Shaykh Naṣr ibn Shaykh ʿAbd al-Bārī ibn al-Ḥājj Muḥammad ibn al-Ḥājj ʿAbd al-Jalīl ibn al-Ḥājj ʿAbd al-Salām al-Ashmawiyyah[1] whose lineage goes back to Ḥasan al-Ashmāwiyyah. He is buried in the west part of the village of Ashmā, located in the protected providence of Manūfiyyah, and completed this work to benefit himself and anyone Allah wills after him, on Thursday, 14 Dhū al-Ḥijjah 1169 AH.

May the best prayers and the purest greetings be upon the Messenger ﷺ, and all praise is due to Allah ﷻ, the Lord of the worlds. May Allah the most High benefit us from the efforts of the author. Āmīn, O Lord of the worlds.

---

(1)   Publisher: We have retained this note so that readers may know the name of the scribe whose manuscript we particularly relied upon for this translation. We do so for the sole purpose of keeping alive his work, effort, and legacy by name and deed. Pray for him and remember him and his family by name.

قَالَ الْمُصَنِّفُ - وَسَّعَ اللهُ مَضْجَعَهُ وَنَفَعَنَا بِبَرَكَةِ عُلُومِهِ وَالْمُسْلِمِينَ - قَدِ اسْتَرَاحَ الْقَلَمُ عَنْ تَسْوِيدِ هَذِهِ الْوُرَيْقَاتِ فِي ثَالِثِ الثَّالِثِ مِنْ رَابِعِ الثَّالِثَةِ مِنْ ثَانِيَةِ الثَّانِي وَصَلَّى اللهُ عَلَى سَيِّدِنَا مُحَمَّدٍ وَعَلَى آلِهِ وَصَحْبِهِ وَسَلَّمَ.

~ ✦ ~